CENTRE FOR THE STUDY OF
ISLAM AND OTHER FAITHS

CSIOF Bulletin

Issue No. 8/9
2015 – 2016

The Centre for the Study of Islam and Other Faiths.
Melbourne School of Theology
An affiliated college of the Australian College of Theology

CSIOF Bulletin
No 8/9 (2015/6)
ISBN-10:0992476321
ISBN-13:978-0-9924763-2-8

© 2016 Melbourne School of Theology Press. All rights reserved.

Editor
Ruth Nicholls

Assistant Editor
Richard Shumack

Production and Cover Design
Ho-yuin Chan

Publishing Services
Published by MST Press
Thank you to Richard Shumack for his publishing services.

Centre for the Study of Islam and Other Faiths
Melbourne School of Theology
5 Burwood Highway, Wantirna, Victoria, 3152, Australia.
PO Box 6257, Vermont South, Victoria, 3133, Australia
Ph: +61 3 9881 7800, Fax: +61 3 9800 0121
csiof@mst.edu.au, www.mst.edu.au/csiof

People involved in Christian interface with other religions are welcome to submit related articles to the Editor for consideration for publishing in the CSIOF Bulletin.

Opinions and conclusions published in the CSIOF Bulletin are those of the authors and do not necessarily represent the views of the CSIOF or its Editors. The Bulletin is purely an information medium, to inform interested parties of religious trends, discussions and debates. The Bulletin affirms the free expression of the religious convictions of its authors but rejects hatred towards any persons or religious group.

Editorial	5
Features	**8**
What's in a Name? Al Qaida, Terrorism and the Global Jihad	8
Jonathan Cole	
Where do they fit?	18
Ruth Nicholls	
From Muslim Youth Radicalization to Terror Strikes	24
Peter Riddell	
A Story of Two Brothers	29
Richard Shumack	
Reflections on a Chronological Reading of the Qur'an	32
Paul Freeman	
Christian Attitudes to the Prophet Muhammad	42
Mark Beaumont	
The Deaths of Jesus and Muhammad: Implications for Historicity	48
Anthony McRoy	
Communiques	**57**
Evaluating a Local Church's Ministry to Muslims	57
William Anderson	
Magdalena: The use of film to target Muslim women	70
Rebecca Hayman	
Connecting with Muslims	84
Martin Schroeder	
Reflections	**87**
Mission 2 Australian Muslims (M2AM) Conference	87
When Women Speak Colloquium	89
Muslim Christian Panel Report	92
Christian Perspectives on a Buddhist Theme	97
Chee Seng Fah	
Paying a visit to Hare Krishna	103
Janaya Wattie	
Book Reviews	**109**
The Wisdom of Islam and the Foolishness of Christianity	109

Men in Charge?: Rethinking Authority in Muslim Legal Tradition 112
Churchill and the Islamic World 115
Jesus & Muhammad 118

CSIOF News and Activities 121

Notes for Contributors *125*

Editorial

Another bomb blast! Another shooting! This type of news is almost becoming common place. How much longer will the media give it press? Soon our ears will fail to react to the news and those who have been killed, hurt and maimed, unless personal acquaintances, will slip unnoticed into the forgotten world. Yet, currently the news of detonated bombs and pictures of blast sites still strike a chord of grief and bewilderment that there are those who deliberately aim to be destructive. Do such actions surprise us? What is it that prompts our reaction? The atrocity itself? The extent of the damage? The human suffering? Should we be surprised? Even in our own society there are those who feel that some form of destructive action will achieve their ends!

Recently, I was reading about Martin Luther. One of the motivating factors driving Luther was his understanding that the "Last Days" were near and that the Devil, true to his nature, was exercising his powers against the church. Five hundred years have passed. What Luther understood then, still, appears relevant and applicable today. Should we be surprised at what we hear and see happening about us? Yes, because human tragedies should arouse in us that sense of horror while also inviting our compassion and concerned response. On the other hand, no, for surely this is what we should be expecting! The Scriptures indicate that war, lawlessness and violence will continue to increase. Nevertheless, as Christians we need to be alert, ready to give an answer for the hope that is within us. We need to be wise. Hence this particular edition of the CSIOF (now the Arthur Jeffery Centre for the Study of Islam) Bulletin attempts to explore issues relating to terrorism.

Jonathan Cole looks at the way 'terrorist' groups define themselves and the failure of the Western media to grasp the significance of their 'self-naming'. Ruth Nicholls' article, while similar to Cole's in considering 'names' looks at the bases which give rise to the differences within Islam and why Islam is not at peace within itself. Peter Riddell's article continues the theme of terrorism by examining the Islamic foundations for the kidnappings, the beheadings, the atrocities against human beings and the warlike activity in order to claim territory for Islam. This article raises the very serious issue of the role of Muhammad, as the example that the terrorists emulate. Richard Shumack's article, written from personal experience, reflects on how two different understandings of Islam impact a family living within Islam. His article highlights the importance of getting to know our Muslim neighbours to understand their perspective on their religion and their life.

The remaining articles of this edition have a somewhat different focus. Anyone who has attempted to read the Qur'an may well have given up in despair. Freeman's article may help. His is a reflection on reading the Qur'an based on what is considered an accepted chronological order. At the beginning of each section he lists the numbers of the various suras thought to be associated with that particular period of the life of the prophet of Islam. Having read the Qur'an using that schema he adds his personal comments. Mark Beaumont's article provides a brief overview of how Christian academics have viewed the prophet since the well-known Christian Islamicist, Kenneth Cragg published his assessment. What a variety of views there are! Anthony McRoy's article is rather provocative. He evaluates the historical evidence for the deaths of Jesus and Muhammad and using the criteria for evaluating historical evidences announces his conclusion.

The two Communique articles look at Christian ministry to Muslims. One is an evaluation of an inner city attempt which invites thoughtful consideration while the other looks at the film *Magdalena* which seeks to invite women from cultures of shame to consider Jesus Christ.

The Reflection section reports on several conferences related to Christian ministry to Muslims while the remaining articles focus on "Other Faiths". Both are reports of visits to specific religious centres – one a Buddhist temple; the other the Hare Krishna Centre.

The final section includes a number of Book Reviews. The titles of the books reflect their diversity and obviously will have a selective appeal.

This issue of the Bulletin has a rich variety of articles which will provide insights into various aspects of Islam and other Faiths. Some may answer your questions; others may raise questions which require further thought and consideration. Send us your questions: you can be sure that others will also be asking them. Those questions reflect the issues that need our consideration.

This is the last edition of the CSIOF Bulletin in this current format. From 26th April, 2016 the Centre for the Study of Islam and Other Faiths became the Arthur Jeffery Centre for the Study of Islam. The rise of the public face of Islam and the growing interest that that has generated has partly prompted the change. As yet the future format of the Bulletin is to be decided. It is more than likely that it will be a 'web production'.

I trust that this issue of the Bulletin will answer some of your questions while also inviting you to learn more.

Ruth Nicholls
Editor

Features

What's in a Name?
Al Qaida, Terrorism and the Global Jihad

Jonathan Cole[1]

The international community today finds itself locked in a global struggle like none other. Organised groups of Muslim men, of varying size, strength and capability, are seeking to establish Islamic states from Indonesia to Mali through the violent overthrow of regimes in those countries. Like-minded groups are also seeking to establish Islamic states in parts of non-Muslim-majority countries such as the Philippines, India and Russia through armed insurgency. Some of the Muslim groups involved in the struggle, and individuals inspired by them in the West, employ the tactic of terrorism against Western citizens at home and abroad in support of these goals. The West is thus involved in the conflict for two reasons. One is because of the direct threat of terrorism to its citizens. The second is because of calls for support, including in some cases military support, from allied governments in Muslim-majority countries under threat.

> *The conflict is now well into its second decade. Yet there is still a surprising lack of clarity, accuracy and consistency in the language the West uses to describe and talk about its opponent.*

The conflict is now well into its second decade. Yet there is still a surprising lack of clarity, accuracy and consistency in the

---

[1] Jonathan Cole is a PhD student in Christian political theology at St Mark's National Theological Centre, Charles Sturt University, in Canberra. He has an MA in Middle Eastern politics and Islamic theology, is an Arabic speaker and worked as a senior terrorism analyst at the Office of National assessments.

language the West uses to describe and talk about its opponent. The 'enemy' is variably characterised as Islamic terrorists, Islamist terrorists, extremists, fundamentalists, radicals, *takfiris*, *jihadi-salafis* (also *salafi-jihadis*) and Islamo-fascists. The lack of agreed terminology and the deficiency of most terms in use suggest confusion, or at the very least profound disagreement, with respect to how the West understands who and what they are fighting.

The terms listed above all suffer from one of two flaws: they are either too broad or too narrow. The term 'Islamic terrorism' is a case in point: it suffers from both flaws. It combines the religious background of individuals, in this case Muslims, with a specific tactic they employ, namely, terrorism. 'Islamic' is far too broad as it refers without qualification to the more than one billion Muslims in the world. On the other hand, the tactic of terrorism is far too narrow, as many Muslims involved in the conflict will never commit or contribute directly to an act of terrorism, according to any legal definition in operation. In fact, the majority of combatants are more accurately described as being engaged in insurgency. Furthermore, some 'terrorist' groups actually have extensive social welfare and missionary wings, involving teachers and aid workers. Describing them as terrorists is simply inaccurate.

The term 'Islamist terrorism' is better than 'Islamic terrorism', but still has its deficiencies. It attempts to more narrowly define the category 'Muslim' to include only those who actively work towards the Islamisation of societies, thus omitting the many millions of what could be described as 'cultural Muslims', or politically disengaged Muslims. It is true that all the Muslims involved in this struggle in one capacity or another could accurately be described as 'Islamists'. The problem, however, is that not all Islamists employ or condone the use of violence in the pursuit of their Islamist vision, let alone conduct or facilitate actual acts of terrorism.

Jihadi-salafi is the most accurate term currently in use, though it is more popular in academic discourse than popular debate. Salafism is a movement within Islam that seeks to return to an imagined pristine form of the faith practised by the prophet Muhammad and the first several generations of his followers. It rejects the authority of the four orthodox legal schools (Hanbali, Shafi'i, Hanafi and Maliki), which developed and were codified some centuries after Muhammad. Most Muslims today follow one of these schools. Instead, salafis recognise the Qur'an and the Sunnah[2] as the sole authorities for deriving Islamic law and doctrine. Everything added since is considered an accretion to be avoided or removed. Not all salafis employ violence in pursuit of their salafist vision for Muslim societies. The qualifier 'jihadi' is thus added in recognition of an important distinction within salafism: those who employ violence and those who do not. 'Jihadi-salafi' is an accurate description of ISIS, Al Qaida and many other groups involved in the global conflict in question. The problem is that not all of the groups involved are salafist. The majority of what are regarded in the West as either terrorist groups of Islamist insurgents in South Asia, such as the Afghan Taliban, actually belong to the Deobandi[3] school of Islam, which follows the Hanafi school of jurisprudence rejected by salafis. It is worth noting that salafis and Deobandis fight together in the insurgency in Afghanistan, but their theological differences are real and do create friction from time to time, even on the battlefield. Thus *jihadi-salafi* doesn't accurately capture all of the organised groups involved in this global struggle, though it does exclude most groups of Muslims that ought to be excluded in any discussion of the conflict.

> ... many Western commentators have tended to overlook the way that the 'terrorists' actually self-identify and conceptualise their struggle.

Why has an accurate and agreed terminology for describing and discussing the Muslim individuals and groups fighting in this conflict proven so elusive for the West? One straightforward explanation is that many Western commentators have tended to overlook the way that the 'terrorists' actually self-identify and conceptualise their struggle. Muslim combatants are in no doubt about

---

[2] Ed. note: The sunnah (sunna) comprises the verbally transmitted teaching, deeds and sayings of the Prophet which, while not recorded in the Qur'an are considered as having been revealed. Not only are they sources for Islamic theology and law they regulate life and living.

[3] Ed. note: The Deobandi, while having Sufi foundations and also emerging from the Hanafi legal school, developed in India essentially as a reaction against British colonialism. As a movement it has spread widely being comparable in influence to the Al Azhar University in Cairo, Egypt. In their teaching they oppose Western values, call on Muslims to "shed blood" for Allah and show contempt for Jews, Christians and Hindus.

their identity and there is great consistency in the way they describe themselves. They simply refer to themselves as *mujahideen* — those engaged in jihad. A related term in use, though less prevalently, is *jihadi* (jihadist). They generally describe their movement as either *al harakah al jihadiyah* (the jihadist movement) or *al tayyar al jihadi* (the jihadist current). These are used more or less synonymously.

Interestingly, the West has a habit of shortening the names of prominent jihadist groups in a way that inadvertently obscures the role jihad plays in their identity. *Al Qaida*, for example, is not the formal name of the organisation so described. Its actual name in Arabic is *Qaidat al Jihad* (the Jihadist Base or Base of Jihad). Similarly, Al Qaida's Somali affiliate – popularly known in the West as *Al Shabaab* – is actually *Xarakada Mujaahidiinta Alshabaab* in Somali, which, in Somali, means *Movement of the Mujahideen Youth*.

It may also surprise some in the West to learn that, as far as jihadists are concerned, their movement dates back to the 1960s, not 11 September 2001. It was in the latter half of the 1960s that the first jihadist movements emerged out of what is known in Arabic as *al sahwah al Islamiyah*, the Islamic awakening. They initially sought to overthrow what they considered to be apostate regimes in Muslim-majority countries like Egypt and Syria. The jihad against the Soviet Union in Afghanistan in the 1980s internationalised the movement, drawing in *mujahideen* from all over the Muslim world to fight and repel an infidel occupation of Muslim land. It was out of this milieu that Osama bin Laden and Al Qaida emerged. Bin Laden succeeded in directing the attention of some, though not all, jihadists to targeting the US and its allies as a priority from the latter half of the 1990s. His legacy has resulted in many groups today incorporating a mixture of calculated and opportunistic targeting of Western interests into their insurgencies against local regimes.

It is worth noting that the lack of understanding and the gulf in comprehension is mutual. Jihadists conceive their Western opponents as Zionist-crusaders, a term that hardly describes accurately the 'post-Christian' secular states they are fighting, but does clearly demonstrate the religious dimension of their conception of the struggle.

The gulf in terminology, conceptualisation and historical perspective are instructive. In some respects, while the West and jihadists are physically engaged in the same conflict, they are not conceptually engaged in the same conflict. This is not a trivial point. The conceptual disparity raises questions about whether the West has in fact come to terms with those whom it is fighting and the motivations and goals of its opponents.

So why have many in the West avoided adopting the language jihadists use to describe themselves? One possible explanation is that *jihad* is an unambiguously religious term. This creates unique difficulties and sensitivities for the West. Jihad is part doctrine, part worship, part law and part theology for Muslims. Moreover, it is a core part of the faith, not a late addition or obscure area of doctrine. It has played an unbroken, integral role in Islamic history. By using the terminology of jihad, contemporary jihadists are imputing orthodoxy to their actions, and by implication charging Muslims who oppose their actions as unorthodox. Whether the West likes it or not, it is involved in a conflict perceived by its opponents as unambiguously religious.

> ... *Western intellectuals concluded that God was dead many decades ago and there has been a steady decline in participation in organised religion in many parts of the West since. This has resulted in a kind of theological illiteracy in the West — ... a lack of ... knowledge of what theology is and what is involved in doing it.*

This is embarrassing and uncomfortable for many in the West. It has been quite some time since the West found itself involved in a religious war in any meaningful sense of the term. Furthermore, Western intellectuals concluded that God was dead many decades ago and consequently there has been a steady decline in participation in organised religion in many parts of the West since. This has resulted in a kind of theological illiteracy in the West — not in the sense of a lack of knowledge of the precepts and histories of religions that have shaped history, like Christianity, Judaism and Islam, but rather in the sense of a knowledge of what theology is and what is involved in doing it.

The so-called 'post-secular' West, with increasing numbers of atheists in academia, government and the media, tends to favour naturalistic interpretations of religious phenomena. This is hardly surprising. If there is no God, then religious behaviour necessarily can only be explained or understood in such terms, whether biological, psychological, anthropological or otherwise. Thus it is not uncommon to encounter views that interpret the behaviour and motivations of jihadists either as a case of the exploitation of religion to legitimise material ends such as power, wealth, fame, justice, vengeance; or as a response to material grievances such as Western policies, political oppression or poverty. In short, such approaches posit that jihadists are political actors motivated by exclusively political goals.

There are problems with approaching the jihadist phenomenon through an exclusively naturalistic paradigm. It must ignore the reasons jihadists give themselves about who they are and what they are fighting for, and in its place discern their true tacit motivations. One of two assumptions underlies this analysis: either jihadists are ignorant of their true identity, motivations and goals, or they are being deliberately dishonest about them. In the face of the overwhelming and consistent evidence that jihadists conceive themselves in religious terms and have explicit religious goals, such as the implementation of the sharia, it is a difficult case to make. Part of the problem likely stems from the 'privatisation' of religion in the West. This is not a concept familiar to most Muslims. Islam is not a matter of private belief separate and distinct from other domains of life like politics, economics, history and science, for many Muslims and certainly not for jihadists. Thus aspects of the jihadist movement that look political to a Western observer can actually be religious from the point of view of the jihadist, as they do not make the distinction.

It is also uncomfortable for the West for other reasons. The West finds itself in some important counterterrorism alliances with Muslim-majority countries and has its own growing Muslim diasporas. Understandably, it wants to avoid causing unnecessary offense to Muslims who do not support or participate in the jihadist cause, and who are often important and essential resources and partners for combating the threat, particularly the domestic terrorist threat in many Western countries.

Perhaps the most important source of discomfort for the West is that to acknowledge the religious identity, motivations and aims of today's *mujahideen* runs directly counter to an article of faith held since 9/11 that Islam is a religion of peace and that the violence perpetrated by so-called jihadists is based on either a misunderstanding or distortion of true Islamic teachings. This comforting myth creates its own misunderstanding and distortion about the complex sociological and theological realities of Islam in the 21st century. It obscures the fact that there is actually no debate within Islam about whether jihad, in a form involving violence under at least some conditions, is a legitimate part of the religion and an obligation for Muslims. The Qur'an doesn't merely exhort the prophet Muhammad and his followers to fight jihad in certain circumstances, it commands it. The belief that some form of jihad is permissible or demanded as a response to the Israeli occupation of Palestinian land or the Western occupation of Afghanistan is widely held and relatively uncontroversial among Muslim scholars and Muslims in general. What is controversial, is how far the duty to wage jihad extends and the permissible tactics that can be used in the course of jihad. The issue is theological and exegetical: what does the divine command to Muhammad to fight the polytheists in 7th century Mecca, which has been continued and expanded by his successors for centuries, mean for Muslims living in the socio-political realities of the 21st century?

The real issue at hand is the validity or otherwise of the jihadists' interpretation and application of the classical doctrine of jihad to current circumstances.

The real issue at hand is the validity or otherwise of the jihadists' interpretation and application of the classical doctrine of jihad to current circumstances. Contemporary jihadists ground their interpretation and application of jihad in textual sources recognised by all Muslims as authoritative: the Qur'an, the Sunna and classical and contemporary commentaries. They seek to apply this classical doctrine to conditions and circumstances altogether unforeseen at the time the revelation was given to the prophet and unknown to the first generations of the prophet's successors. Such conditions include a world in which there is no caliphate; a reduced area of Muslim domination; a limited number of Muslim-majority countries observing Islamic law (sharia) and increasing numbers of Muslims living in the West under legal codes at odds with important precepts of the sharia.

It is a truism that all sacred texts require interpretation. They don't interpret themselves. It is thus the job of theologians to apply revelation to new situations, contexts and developments as history unfolds. This is not something unique to Islam. Christianity and Judaism face the same challenge of applying scripture to new circumstances and situations. It is not well appreciated in the West that those Muslim scholars who disagree with jihadists and believe that violent jihad is not required or justified modern circumstances, equally rely on theological interpretation to make their case. It is not as simple as just reading the Qur'an and applying the plain meaning of the text. Some interpretation is necessary for Muslims to live in accordance with the Qur'an today.

Therefore, the question doesn't hinge on whether the jihadist interpretation and application of jihad is 'correct' or 'wrong'. It hinges on whether it is valid – that is to say whether the authoritative sources of Islam can be read in such a way that a Muslim could reasonably conclude that jihad is either commanded or permitted in response to at least some current geo-political developments (which may or may not have been explicitly envisaged in the texts or have been confronted by Muslims previously). At a more basic level, the authority of a particular interpretation is determined largely in part by its ability to win support from Muslims. Proportionally small, but significant, numbers of Muslims find the jihadist interpretation compelling.

It is important to note that the issue is not whether the jihadists have the only valid understanding of jihad. It is a simple matter of empirical fact that the interpretation of today's *mujahideen* is not the only one extant. It is not even the most popular or prevalent one within Islam. However, the fact that it might be empirically-speaking a minority view is immaterial to the question of its validity or otherwise. Moreover, its minority status does not belie the fact that it is having a strategic impact and has grown in influence in recent decades.

The notion that the jihadist interpretation and application of jihad is valid might go a long way to explaining why it is proving so difficult for 'moderate' Islam to 'de-legitimise' extremist elements in their midst. If jihadists in fact were 'distorting' or 'perverting' Islamic scripture and traditions, it ought to be relatively straightforward for moderates to demonstrate this and thus de-legitimise their claims. But what we have witnessed is a steady, albeit modest, growth in extremism over the last decade, not a diminution. The problem is not that moderate Muslims and scholars do not have valid arguments for a much more constrained understanding and application of jihad. Such arguments exist. The problem is that such interpretations of jihad can only offer alternatives to extremist interpretations, rather than invalidations of their arguments.

It is time the West abandoned the pretence that the conflict it finds itself in has nothing to do with the religion of Islam and that there is absolutely no validity whatsoever to the jihadists' interpretation and application of jihad. This myth is not a prerequisite for building harmonious Western societies which include Muslims. Moreover, acknowledging the link between Islam and jihad, made daily by jihadists themselves, is not the same as asserting that Islam is a religion of violence or that all Muslims are violent and therefore a threat. But the inescapable reality is that one religious community, in this case Islam, is generating a unique set of threats to Western lives and interests that no other community is, whether religious, ethnic or ideological. Greater honesty about the complex, though inextricable, link between the religion of Islam and the global conflict with contemporary jihadism would force more Muslim scholars to directly confront some difficult theological questions about jihad. The influence of moderate scholars prevailing in Muslim discourse about the meaning of jihad for Muslims today is ultimately the best hope for dealing with the threat from modern jihadists. Pretending, or perhaps hoping, that there is no validity to the theology of contemporary jihadists, is not a viable counterterrorism strategy.

> *The problem is not that moderate Muslims and scholars do not have valid arguments for a much more constrained understanding and application of jihad. Such arguments exist. The problem is that such interpretations of jihad can only offer alternatives to extremist interpretations, rather than invalidations of their arguments.*

Finally, while the West is not a legitimate party to internal Muslim theological debates, it shouldn't use that as an excuse to avoid investigation and analysis of the theological dimensions of the issue. Western analysis of jihadists would benefit from a more phenomenological approach that took seriously the religious motivations and aspirations of jihadists as jihadists articulate them. It is a dictum of war to know your enemy. The West needs to become literate in Islamic scripture and theology if it hopes to understand whom and what it is fighting.

Where do they fit?
Differences within Islam

Ruth Nicholls[1]

Ahmadiyyas, Ismailis, Wahhabi, Salafi, ISIS, Sufi, Shi'a, Sunni? Heard those words? What about Catholic, Anglican, Methodist, Presbyterian, Baptist, Jehovah's Witnesses, Seventh Day Adventists, Christian Science? No doubt, this last group of words is more familiar. Each of this latter group has some connection with Christianity. But the question we might ask is, how Christian are they? How one defines 'what is Christianity', will determine 'how Christian one considers a particular group'. For many years, for example, the Catholics would not recognise Protestants as 'Christian' and vice versa (and that still occurs to some degree today). 'Christian Science' would certainly be considered on the outer – for some neither Christian nor science. Most Christians would consider the teaching of the Jehovah's Witnesses as a heresy and are perhaps not sure about the Seventh Day Adventists. Also, let's not forget that Christians have had their day in 'killing' those whom they consider 'heretics'. To use a 'modern term', Christians too have also created refugee problems. The Huguenots fled France to escape persecution from 'Christians' in the 17th Century; the Pilgrim Fathers fled to America to escape persecution from 'Christians' in Europe. All of which is cause for some sombre reflection.

But why such an introduction? Let's revisit the list of names with which we began: Ahmadiyyas, Ismailis, Wahhabi, Salafi, ISIS, Sufi, Shi'a, Sunni? What do these names have in common?

---

[1] Dr Ruth Nicholls spent many years in an Islamic country and is currently the Administrator for Melbourne School of Theology Arthur Jeffery Centre for the Study of Islam, formerly the Centre for the Study of Islam and Other Faiths.

Each of these groups claim *Allah* as their God, the *Qur'an* as their Holy Book, and also recite the Muslim creed, formally called the *shahada* or testimony, "I bear witness that there is no god but Allah and that Muhammad is God's messenger". Each of these groups observe the five pillars of Islam, the creed, the *salat* (the five times a day prayer cycle), the fast, *zakat* (a religious tax, a type of charity), the hajj (the pilgrimage to Mecca at least once in one's life time) and believe in *jihad*.[2] Yet, despite the allegiance of these different groups to what can be considered the fundamentals of Islam, in many Islamic countries these different groups are often violently opposed to one another. The December 2015 bomb blast in the predominantly Shi'ite, Parachinnar area in NW Pakistan appears to have been carried out by a Sunni related terrorist group. Other examples include the recent bombing of the mosques in Medina, Jeddah and Qatif in Saudi Arabia[3] as well as the bombing of the training centre in Aden, in Yemen in August 2016[4]. In addition, since 1974 the Ahmadiyyas have been legally declared 'non-Muslims'.

> *What is it about humanity that demands 'blood' when people hold different views (ideals, beliefs) to one's own?*

Why is it that even within a family, when there is an emotionally heated controversy over someone adopting a 'different point of view' to the one traditionally held, it can result in separation, estrangement and, in some cases death? What is it about humanity that demands 'blood' when people hold different views (ideals, beliefs) to one's own? Indeed, a study of history shows that when people hold 'opposing views' that are not accepted by 'others' then the result can be 'bloodshed'. While the issue has been raised, the answer is not the focus here. The purpose of this paper is to consider the different claims of these Islamic groups to discover why Islam, 'the religion of Peace', is at times, at war within itself.

---

[2] However, each of the groups may express their understanding of what *jihad* entails somewhat differently. While usually understood in a military sense it can also be understood in a more personal sense as one's own personal struggle.

[3] http://www.aljazeera.com/news/2016/07/saudi-arabia-qatif-explosion-160704165007140.html cited 4 August, 2016

[4] http://www.aljazeera.com/news/2016/08/deadly-suicide-bombing-targets-yemen-army-camp-160829064018700.html 30th August, 2016 cited 30 August, 2016

Given the confines of this paper, this will be an overview which will provide a basic understanding of the bases for controversy, while providing a framework for further exploration.

During Muhammad's lifetime (b. 570CE) commencing at about 610 and then for some twenty years, Muslims believe that their prophet had revelations from God, via Gabriel, which he recited to those around him. At the time they were not recorded in any concise or organised manner, but circulated primarily in oral form, though some did get written down. Although having gathered together a band of followers, opposition to his teaching resulted in Muhammad leaving Mecca. In 622 he was invited by the oasis town of Yathrib (Medina) to become an arbiter of their disputes. (This incident (*hijra*) is often considered as the beginning of Islam and the Islamic calendar counts its years from this event.) His followers joined him and from there Muhammed was able to extend his political power and influence. From this base in Medina, Muhammad was involved in a significant number of military encounters including one in which the Meccans surrendered without fighting (629/630).

Leadership

The Prophet of Islam, Muhammad died in about 632. Since Muhammad had made no succession plans the question of leadership naturally arose, and was to continue for some years. It was during the rule of the fourth and last "rightly guided caliph" that the issue of leadership resulted in the 'assassination' of that caliph Ali. It is at this point that a significant difference arose. The Sunnis who claim to be the 'true followers' of Muhammad followed the victor while Shi'ites consider that it was Ali 'who was the rightful leader'. Then, later, within the Shi'a community further issues relating to leadership developed which led to various offshoots of which the Ismailis are one.

During his lifetime, Muhammad established himself as the leader and claimed divine authority for his position as the Prophet of Islam. Those who surrounded him at that time, or to use the Arabic expression 'sat on the seat' with him were considered the 'true followers' of Islam and the 'holders of the Islamic truths': the Sunnis. So then it is not surprising that there are those within the scope of Islam that emphasise their relationship to this original group. The Wahhabis, the Salafi and ISIS would consider themselves to belong to this group. This group would claim that they, and only they, have the true understanding of Islam and that their understanding is the one that must be practised. Of these the Wahhabis, the Salafi and ISIS are attempts to reform Islam and bring it back to the splendour and glory it experienced during the early years of its existence.

The Revelation

The illiterate Muhammad did not personally record the revelations he received in a book. Muslims believe that these revelations were collated into the present Qur'anic form between 650 and 656 some twenty or so years after his death. While various collations were circulating at the time, the Caliph Uthman demanded that other versions be destroyed and that his version be considered the accepted one. In addition, it is said that Uthman settled the way that the Arabic text should be read. Nevertheless, especially among non-Muslim scholars, issues regarding the recording and compilation of the Qur'an continue to surface.

As with any Holy Book, questions of understanding and interpretation or exegesis arise and that is also true for the Qur'an. Those who interpret the Qur'an are called *muffasir* while the interpretation is called *tafsir*. Not surprisingly, differences in interpretation and understanding are reflected in and give rise to the various groups that occur within Islam. However, the interpretation and understanding tend to follow the known branches within Islam such as Sunni, Shi'a and Ahmadiyya. Often it would seem that there has been little attempt to reconcile these differences. As is so often the case with humanity, the stance that 'my belief is right and yours is wrong and you must adhere to mine or suffer the consequences' comes into play.

Interpreting the Law - Sharia

In addition, the Qur'an is also considered to be the source of law *sharia* together with the hadith (the recorded sayings) and actions of the Prophet (*sunna*). Establishing what is the 'actual' law and how it is to be observed in the current context is called jurisprudence (*fiqr*). Again, the various branches of Islam have developed their own 'schools'. The Sunnis recognise four schools, Hanabi, Hanafi, Maliki and Shafi'i while the Shi'ite have one.

The life and the sayings of the Prophet
There is yet another facet which gives rise to differences of interpretation and practice. While Muslims believe the Qur'an records the revelations of the prophet by the angel Gabriel, the prophet was asked many questions and his advice on various issues was also sought. Many of these responses were remembered and have been gathered together in various collections called the *Hadith*. The validity of a 'hadith' depends upon the record of its recollection and the reputation of the person(s) who recited it. Not surprisingly then, the various groups within Islam accept or reject a hadith on the basis of their own scale of reference. So while one group might hold strongly to a 'saying' of the Prophet, another group may reject it. The most accepted collections for the Sunni are those *Sahih al-Bukhari* and *Sahih Muslim*. The Shi'a have their own collection of hadith.

Beside the Qur'an and the Hadith, the life (*sira*) and the practice(s) of the Prophet (*sunna*) are another source which influences Muslim life and practice to varying degrees depending upon the perceived value of the record.

The Sufis, on the other hand, are the mystics of Islam reflecting its 'emotional heart'. Rejected by the Orthodox who emphasise 'adherence and practice', Sufism aims to fulfil the 'law and the spirit' of the Qur'an and the hadith. Sufis follow a more mystical or esoteric interpretation of the Qur'an. The use of mystical practices in many countries has often resulted in the absorption of local practices into Islam fostering the growth of folk Islam. Not surprisingly, the Sufis in general as well as the practitioners of folk Islam are often considered heretical by those who consider themselves more orthodox. As a consequence, in a number of instances, Sufis have become the target of the wrath of those who do not consider them to hold to 'orthodox Islam'. An example of this was the bombing of a very famous Sufi saint complex in Lahore, in Pakistan some years ago.

> *Put these differences together with that seeming human necessity to demand that 'you believe what I believe or else', it is not surprising that currently Islam is at war within itself.*

The Ahmadiyya is a more modern expression of Islam which is strongly rejected by other sections of Islam. Again the issue centres primarily on a question of interpretation and an understanding of the Qur'an. Mirza Ghulam Ahmed believed that he was divinely appointed as the Mahdi, the person who was going to follow the prophet and bring in a new era of Islam. This interpretation and understanding is rejected by the more orthodox interpretations of Islam, with the result that the Ahmadiyya have been declared non-Muslims and are virtually stateless within the Islamic Republic of Pakistan.

Conclusion

So then, the bases for the differences that have given rise to the various groups within Islam revolve around questions of leadership; the interpretation of the Qur'an and the resultant practices which also are reflected in and influenced by the particular understanding or *tafsir* of the Qur'an, the particular 'school of jurisprudence' followed; the acceptance or rejection of *Hadith*. Put these differences together with that seeming human necessity to demand that 'you believe what I believe or else', it is not surprising that currently Islam is at war within itself. Add to that fact that within Islam there are those who claim one or more of the above bases together with a particular Qur'anic verse(s) and/or *hadith* as a validation for their belief and as 'the right understanding' which becomes the justification for killing those who do not hold to their interpretation and practice.

From Muslim Youth Radicalization to Terror Strikes

Peter Riddell[1]

Terrorism was seen at its worst in 2015 in Paris. The year began with the murder of twelve people at the offices of the magazine *Charlie Hebdo*, targeted by young Muslim radicals for its various published satires on Muhammad and Islam. On the same day a Jewish kosher supermarket was taken over by an associate of the *Charlie Hebdo* attackers, and four Jewish shoppers were murdered. Then Muslim radicalism struck with devastating effect on the evening of Friday 13 November, when 129 people were murdered and more than 300 wounded by a team of young Muslim radicals. Islamic State and Al-Qaeda claimed responsibility for the various attacks.

All the terrorist attackers were in their 20s or 30s. Most were French or Belgian citizens. At least one had arrived in Greece and registered as a refugee.

An obvious question that arises from the above details is the motivation of such young Muslim terrorists. US Secretary of State John Kerry offers an answer:

> "They are in fact psychopathic monsters and there is nothing, nothing civilized about them. So this is not a case of one civilization pitted against another. This is a battle between civilization itself and barbarism and fascism. Both at the same time."[2]

---

[1] Peter Riddell serves as Vice Principal Academia and Senior Research Fellow in Islam at the Melbourne School of Theology. He has published extensively on Islam and Christian-Muslim Relations.

[2] http://www.politico.com/story/2015/11/john-kerry-paris-visit-215941 cited 10 December, 2015

This analysis is wildly off-target, completely ignoring any religious dimension to the motivation of Muslim terrorists. The fact that a US government official of Kerry's stature and influence could so misunderstand the situation is itself a matter of great concern.

What are the factors that lead young Muslim men to undertake such violent acts, and what are the factors that are driving so many other young Muslims to commit themselves to fight for the Islamic State caliphate?

Elements in the radicalization process

There is a central idea fuelling Muslim youth radicalization: young Muslims travelling this path are following a particular conceptual **role model** that praises activism for Islam, jihadi militancy and death for the sake of Allah. A range of intersecting elements underlie this core idea.

The first is the problem of radical preachers in some mosques, as revealed in the "Undercover Mosque" series of documentaries produced for *Dispatches* in the UK some years ago.[3] It is very likely that some mosques and their preachers attended by the Paris attackers, especially in the Molenbeek area of Brussels, were a source of some of their radical ideas.

> *There is a central idea fuelling Muslim youth radicalization: young Muslims travelling this path are following a particular conceptual **role model** that praises activism for Islam, jihadi militancy and death for the sake of Allah*

The subversive role of such preachers is exacerbated by easy access to radical Islamic websites and social media sites. Jihadi groups such as Islamic State are very skilled at hooking impressionable young minds through social media. From time to time such sites are banned by governments but others quickly emerge in their place. Such websites create the ingredients for a further key element reinforcing a radicalized role model: a peer group of real life and virtual radicalized youth which adds fuel to the pressures on young Muslims.

---

[3] https://vimeo.com/19598947 cited 10 December, 2015

Sadly, parents sometimes also provide a radicalized role model. The father of one of the much discussed 15-year-old jihadi brides from Bethnal Green in London who joined Islamic State in Syria was filmed taking a very active part in one protest led by the notorious radical preacher Anjem Choudary.[4] Many young Muslims are brought up in family contexts where rabid anti-Westernism is a key part of family discourse. This is likely to have been the case in the Abdeslam family which provided two of the participants in the Paris attacks.

A further and crucial role model for radicalization for young Muslims is provided by the prophet of Islam himself. Muhammad is a complex character, but during the last 10 years of his life in the city of Medina, Islamic sources, such as the prophetic traditions or *Hadith*, and the authoritative biography of Muhammad or *Sira*, record that he developed the doctrine of jihad, plundered trading caravans, sanctioned the beheading of perceived enemies, and endorsed forced concubinage.

How to respond to the radicalization process
So what can be done to prevent the radicalization of Muslim youth in the West, and thereby to prevent attacks such as took place in Paris? To some extent, responses can be linked with the above factors producing radicalization.

First, there should be a mechanism for monitoring sermons in mosques which have a history of questionable preaching. This practice is already followed in some countries in the world, including Muslim countries, such as in Singapore, Pakistan, and Egypt.[5]

Second, radical preachers should be prosecuted and, where possible, deported, as was the case with Abu Qatada who was expelled from the UK to Jordan,[6] and Abu Hamzah al-Masri, who

---

[4] http://www.dailymail.co.uk/news/article-3013703/Father-jihadi-bride-schoolgirl-attended-2012-Islamist-rally-attended-Lee-Rigby-s-killer-led-preacher-Anjem-Choudary.html cited 10 December, 2015

[5] http://www.dawn.com/news/1184519 cited 10 December, 2015

[6] http://www.bbc.com/news/uk-23213740 cited 10 December, 2015

was extradited from the UK to the United States to face terrorism charges.[7] At the same time, western governments should take steps to limit access to radical websites. Civil libertarians will be uncomfortable with any suggestion of censorship, but these are unusual problems that require extraordinary solutions.

Furthermore, citizenship should be withdrawn from dual nationals found guilty of involvement in radical groups, as is being explored by Australia and France.[8] This should also apply to parents involved in radicalization of their children. At the same time, there is an urgent need for re-education programs for returning jihadis and their brides.

Finally, moderate Muslim leadership needs to address the elephant in the room: the role of Muhammad as a model for jihadi activism. This issue is barely touched upon in public discourse and, when it is broached, it is usually addressed in hushed tones and from an oblique angle. But there is little doubt that radical Muslim youth look ultimately to the example of their prophet during his years in Medina. It cries out for a full and free discussion.

> No other marginalized religious minority community produces hostile and radicalized youth in this way. Islam is a special case, a fact that should be acknowledged and acted upon by church and state alike.

As for Christian responses, the church must work with government and other social institutions in addressing this crisis along the above lines. The potent cocktail of ingredients that lead young Muslim youth down the path of radicalization puts paid to a simplistic explanation that has been popular amongst church people; namely, that Muslim youth radicalization simply results from their alienation from majority society, which must bear the major responsibility for the result. No other marginalized religious minority community produces hostile and radicalized youth in this

---

[7] http://www.bbc.com/news/world-us-canada-30754959 cited 10 December, 2015

[8] http://www.abc.net.au/news/2015-05-26/government-promises-laws-to-strip-citizenship-from-terrorists/6498300; http://www.thelocal.fr/20151006/france-to-strip-nationality-from-five-terrorists cited 10 December, 2015

way. Islam is a special case, a fact that should be acknowledged and acted upon by church and state alike.

A Story of Two Brothers[1]

Richard Shumack[2]

The two brothers

In close to twenty years of ministry with Muslims I have only received one personal death threat and it was from one of the nicest Muslims I have met! Here's how it happened. I had been speaking about Jesus for a while with a young Muslim man. He didn't take his Muslim faith very seriously. Indeed, he would have called himself a "bad" Muslim and he clearly lived a life that contravened Muslim law. Nevertheless, he still believed in God and because he had some health issues that worried him he was more than happy to consider the possibility that Jesus had something to offer to him (many Muslims are happy to recognize Jesus as a healer).

One time I went to visit him in his home where I met his older brother. The older brother was an honest, gentle young man who was very passionate about his faith and fervent in his longing for justice in the world – especially for his suffering Muslim brothers and sisters. Based on his reading of the Qur'an and Muslim tradition he was fully, if reluctantly, prepared to use force to achieve this justice where necessary, if he believed God was calling him to it. When he discovered that his younger brother and I had been talking about Jesus he very gently and compassionately warned me that I'd better

> ... for the sake of everyone Islam should be defended at all costs.

---

[1] This article first appeared in the CMS *Checkpoint*, Summer 2015\16, p5,6 and reproduced here with permission.

[2] Dr Richard Shumack is the Director the Arthur Jeffery Centre for the Study of Islam formerly the Centre for the Study of Islam and Other Faiths at Melbourne School of Theology. He is also part of the *Understanding and Answering Islam* team, Ravi Zacharias International Ministries. Richard did his doctorate in Islamics at Melbourne University. He was also a short term missionary in Cairo with his wife.

stop. This was because on the very slim chance that his brother converted to Christianity then he would have to kill me. He made it very clear that, since he liked me, he would rather not kill me, but that for the sake of everyone, Islam should be defended at all costs. This single incident highlights many of the opportunities, as well as the challenges, in Christian ministry to Muslims.

> ... *the Muslim vision of a just world – one in which peace and justice reigned through all having submitted perfectly to the [Sharia] laws*

This incident brings out the range of belief and practice that one encounters in Islam. The older brother displayed the passionate faith of keen traditional Muslims in his deep longing to be both personally righteous and right with God. This longing, however, could only be expressed through obedience to Allah's beautiful and just laws (the Sharia). He actively pursued the Muslim vision of a just world – one in which peace and justice reigned through *all* having submitted perfectly to these laws. Moreover, he had fully embraced a conservative political Islamism in which appropriate force (like police and army, rather than random acts of terrorism) can properly be utilized in the enforcement of these laws – upon even those who don't believe (for their own sake). It is this style of Islam that we see gaining ground in the Middle East – most extremely in the case of I.S. At the same time, it is important to recognize that the older brother's strict faith was a minority position, in both his family and his wider community. He was the "religious" one – a point of both public pride and private eye-rolling.

The younger brother on the other hand represented what in my experience is the majority position in Islam: that the sharia might be theologically true, but it is experientially burdensome, unrealistic and unsatisfying. They identify as Muslim, sometimes very strongly, but that is because their community is called "Muslim". Beyond the very basics to do with prayer, Ramadan, and giving, their personal beliefs often bear very little relation to traditional orthodoxy. Unsurprisingly they have no interest in political Islam – indeed many are running away from it towards a more experientially satisfying vision of human flourishing. Many even conceive of God in mystical ways that bear far closer resemblance to the personal and relational God of the Bible than to the supremely transcendent Allah of the Qur'an.

My interaction with both brothers revealed the extraordinary opportunities, and occasional challenges, that Muslims offer for sharing Jesus. They are theists who believe in a God who creates, sustains and judges with mercy and righteousness. They are conscious that this life is not all that there is and they are willing to take a public stand on issues of social justice and community morality. Importantly, they are more than happy to speak about God and their experience of faith. In fact, like nearly all Muslims I have met, they are far more willing to speak about God than most Christians! Challenges – and even risks – remain though. The small percentage of Islamists pressure their Muslim brothers and sisters to reject Christ, and sometimes this becomes forceful. Threats, like the one I experienced, exist, and Christians need to renounce fear and embrace the grace and boldness of Christ that enables us to love even our enemies.

> *In fact, like nearly all Muslims I have met, they are far more willing to speak about God than most Christians!*

> *Like in Luke, one of my brothers was a super obedient legalist with a strong sense of religious duty and the other was a disobedient and messed up rebel who lived at the fringes of his community. Also like Luke, neither of the brothers had any real sense of what their father – their heavenly father – was like.*

In so many ways, my story of the two brothers reminded me of Jesus' own story of two brothers in Luke 15. Like in Luke, one of my brothers was a super obedient legalist with a strong sense of religious duty and the other was a disobedient and messed up rebel who lived at the fringes of his community. Also like Luke, neither of the brothers had any real sense of what their father – their heavenly father – was like. One tried to impress God with faithful obedience and law enforcement; the other languished in brokenness with the desperate, but unrealistic, hope that redemption might be possible. The most urgent need of both was to know their heavenly Father who had run to earth in Christ to offer them the satisfying life and the beautiful world they had been seeking.

Reflections on a Chronological Reading of the Qur'an

Paul Freeman[1]

Editor: Because the chapters (sura) of the Qur'an are not ordered chronologically in most editions, a reader who reads from beginning to end will miss out on the sequence of Muhammad's life which is reportedly contained in the Qur'an. In order to grasp that sequence, readers need first to read the Meccan chapters, in the order of their compiling, and then read the Medinan chapters which reflect the last ten years of Muhammad's life. One generally accepted chronology was proposed by Theodor Nöldeke. Paul Freeman provides a series of reflections on an initial reading of the Qur'an according to this well-regarded chronology. (The appropriate chapters are listed at the beginning of each section.) In reading the Qur'an it should be noted that God/Allah uses the personal pronouns such as "I, me, we, us".

Reflections on the Suras from the First Meccan Period
96, 74, 111, 106, 108, 104, 107, 102, 105, 92, 90, 94, 93, 97, 86, 91, 80, 68, 87, 95, 103, 85, 73, 101, 99, 82, 81, 53, 84, 100, 79, 77, 78, 88, 89, 75, 83, 69, 51, 52, 56, 70, 55, 112, 109, 113, 114, 1

In reading through the Qur'an for the first time in my life, I had many expectations. Firstly, that I would be able to have some context for passages which completely baffle me. One of these is 3:44:

> "You were not present among them when they cast lots to see which of them should take charge of Mary, you were not present with them when they argued about her."

---

[1] Paul Freeman is a pseudonym. Paul works with a Muslim majority people group in Africa. He is married, has three children and is currently pursuing his Masters in Muslim Studies.

I wonder if verses such as these are akin to 1 Pet. 3:19, when Jesus "preached to the spirits who were in prison," which is an odd detail that no one knows for certain what is meant. Are there many deep details like this, or is this a characteristic of the mystery in the revelations that Muhammad is relaying? Secondly, I hoped to see how particularly special this book is, and how it presents the Supreme Being.

> *In reading the first Meccan suras, one of my first surprising observations was the frequent reference to judgment*

In reading the first Meccan suras, one of my first surprising observations was the frequent reference to judgment. God is almost presented as a Being who eagerly desires to throw sinful beings into hell, anticipating their recompense for their bad behaviour.

"He has been stubbornly hostile to Our revelation: I will inflict a mounting torment on him…I will throw him into the scorching Fire" (74:16, 17, 26).

On this topic, I was surprised at how often in his first Meccan period suras on final judgment and the flames or torment of hell are mentioned.

My first response is to postulate that Muhammad's strategy to get people to follow his teaching was a scare tactic. My second thought was that the lack of development in teaching something other than judgment and hell shows that he was not as interested in developing a new religion as may have seemed. Rather, he was wanting his people to move out of their backward polytheistic practices and join with the philosophy of those he looked up to, perhaps, the "People of the Book" and the Jews.

I also noticed that suras 99, 82 and 84 are strikingly similar: they begin describing an earthquake of some sort. The earth is then personified and brings forth its dead who are then judged. Other suras include part of this imagery, such as sura 100, which also mentions, "the contents of the earth are thrown out," (v.9) and judged. A number of other suras detail changing planetary and earthly developments before the final judgment, such as 77: 1-13, 69:13-18, 70:8-9, and 56:1-6.

During this early Meccan period this final judgment is often repeated and seems to be the crux of his message. Specific details include: a trumpet sounding (74:8-9); no one knowing the hour of judgment except God (79:42-44); those deemed evil being thrown into hell, which will not only be for the evildoers (82:14) but also for those who are distracted by the world (102:1-8) as well as those negligent of good deeds (101:8, 107:1-6).

Another recurring theme is the humbleness of the origin of man, that he was made from a small helpless form: a "clinging form" (96:2), "a spurting fluid" (86:6), "a droplet" (80:19), "a drop of spilt-out sperm, which became a clinging form" (75:37-38), "an ejected drop of sperm" (53:46); and "dried clay, like pottery" (55:14).

My last comment relates to the Qur'an as the uncreated, eternal word of God—an attribute that Christians do not ascribe to the Bible. In reading these first Meccan suras, I was struck by how human the style and discourse sounded. Sura 55, for example, is so poetic and rhythmic. If God is wholly other, and his uncreated eternal word is the Qur'an, how does it fit so well into human culture? We must maintain that the Qur'an itself must reflect to a degree that God is other and separate from us.

> If God is wholly other, and his uncreated eternal word is the Qur'an, how does it fit so well into human culture?

Secondly, how is it that an eternal, uncreated written thing can reference something that is created and did have a beginning? In eternity past, for example, how did the word "pregnant camels" in 81:4 have any meaning before camels even existed? I realize that I must rest this line of critique in the knowledge of the unknowable mystery of God, and that just as I cannot truly fathom the Trinity, the omnipresence of God and how He exists outside of time and space, so I must grant my Muslim friend understanding in the difficulty of expressing divine mysteries, like the confusing nature of the uncreated Qur'an. At least, when a Muslim friend argues against the confusing nature of the Trinity, we can point out that there are likewise confounding aspects in his beliefs.

Reflections on the Suras from the Second Meccan Period
54, 37, 71, 76, 44, 50, 20, 26, 15, 19, 38, 36, 43, 72, 67, 23, 21, 25, 17, 27, 18

The second Meccan period suras bring new elements to the Qur'anic message. The most notable one is reference to Biblical characters such as Moses (37:114-122; 44:17-33; 20:9-98; 26:10-68; 19:51-53; 43:46-56; 23:45-49; 21:48-50; 25:35-36; 17:101-104); Noah (54:9-15; 37:75-82; 71:1-28; 26:105-122; 23:23-30; 21:76-77; 25:37); Abraham (37:83-113; 26:69-89; 15:57-60; 19:41-50; 38:45 43:26; 21:51-70); Adam (20:115-123; 15:26-50; 17:61); Lot (54:33-40; 37:133-138; 26:160-175; 15:61-77; 21:71-75; 27:54-58); Job (38:41-44; 21:83-84); David and Solomon (38:17-26, 30-40; 21:78-82; 27:15-44); Mary and Jesus (19:16-34; 43:57-60; 23:50; 21:91); Zechariah (19:1-15; 21:89-90); Jonah (37:139-148; 21:87-88) and Ishmail (19:54-55; 21:85). In many of these suras, the use of the stories of Biblical prophets, whose messages were taunted and ridiculed by the people, is to encourage Muhammad. They show how he, like the earlier prophets, suffered in the same ways (21:41, 25:4-6), including opposition by those who thought Muhammad was bewitched (17:47). God's message to Muhammad is that he should keep on warning even though he is just "a lone man" (54:23) chosen from among his own people (38:4) and not an angel (25:7).

Another new emphasis in the second Meccan period suras is the idea of God's mercy. Frequently, God is referred to as "Lord of Mercy" (43:36, 45, 81; 17:110; 23:75; 67:3, 19, 29; 36:5, 16, 52), and that God is "most merciful" (23:109, 118; 21:36, 42, 83; 25:59, 70; 27:11). I also noted some examples of how God is merciful (17:66ff and 18:58-59), including that the Qur'an itself is a mercy (17:82). On the other hand, we also read about God withholding mercy (23:75-77), leading some to stray (18:17b) and appointing adversaries for prophets (25:31).

> ... the second Meccan suras bring new elements to the Qur'anic message

Overall, the overwhelming chorus echoing throughout the second Meccan period suras seems to be one of warning disbelievers of coming judgment and hell (54:6-8; 37:19-39; 71; 76:4; 44:10-16; 50:20-30; 20:15-16,74, 100-111; 26:90-104; 19:37-39, 97-98; 38:14-17; 36:48-65; 43:65-67; 72:15, 23-28; 67:6-11;

23:63-67, 101-104; 21:29; 25:11-14, 26-29; 17:8, 18, 63, 97-99; 27:90; 18:29, 52, 106). So central is this warning to the message of the Qur'an (at least in this section) that almost every chapter alludes to the coming judgment! At first, I found it paradoxical that there is such an emphasis on judgment when there is also a strong emphasis, as previously noted, on God as the Lord of mercy. The solution to understanding this paradox, perhaps, is in the mercy of the Qur'an itself, since

> "Never have We destroyed a town without sending down messengers to warn it" (26:208).

The Qur'an speaks of itself as a mercy that could have been taken away (17:86-87).

> *It seems that Muslims are more concerned about devotion and purity in the general community than personal relationship.*

One aspect of God's message that I expected to find much more frequently in the Qur'an was general instructions about how a person should live with his neighbour. I was interested to finally find a small section that addresses this in 17:22-38. The uniqueness of this passage from the message of the majority of the text through this period makes me wonder if this reflects the aloof, other, distant, unconcerned nature of God that I sense is perceived by my Muslim friends. It seems that Muslims are more concerned about devotion and purity in the general community than personal relationship. This can also be seen in how God permits Job to strike his wife to carry out what he had promised on oath when he was relieved of his suffering in 38:44 (see M.A.S. Abdel Haleem's note on this verse for its context). We can learn from this verse that after making what should be interpreted as a foolish oath on Job's part, God is more concerned that he fulfils his oath rather than from keeping Job from striking his wife.

My last observation on this section is the remarkable similarity that 20:105-112 has with Isaiah 40:3-5. Besides the numerous references to Biblical characters as previously noted, I wonder to what extent Muhammad had access to the Bible. From previous reading, I understand that there was no Arabic Bible in the 6th and 7th centuries and Muhammad, in any case, was illiterate.

However, a Christian or Jew could have recited Isaiah 40 as well as stories of the prophets and Jesus to him using a rough translation.

Reflections on the Suras from the Third Meccan Period

32, 41, 45, 16, 30, 11, 14, 12, 40, 28, 39, 29, 31, 42, 10, 34, 35, 7, 46, 6, 13

> *The third Meccan period suras are significantly distinct from the previous two periods in three ways.*

The third Meccan period suras are significantly distinct from the previous two periods in three ways: a development in the description of the nature of God; further developments in the understanding of the final judgment; and a development in the perception of Muhammad's prophethood.

In the third Meccan period suras, the development of understanding the nature of God is achieved by using two adjectives usually appearing as a 'pair' which occur at the end of a story or a statement. These two adjectives make a statement about the nature of God. For example:

> "All that rests by night or by day belongs to him. He is the All Hearing, the All Knowing" (6:13),

and

> "No one will receive any help except for those to whom God shows mercy: He is the Mighty, the Merciful Lord" (46:42).

Not every attribute of God mentioned in this way necessarily relates to the subject of the preceding ideas, for example:

> "He has subjected the sun and moon to run their courses for an appointed time; He is truly the Mighty, the Forgiving" (39:5).

Other descriptive comments about God that I noted in reading the suras of this period include the following:

- the God of the 'People of the Book,' the Christians, is the same as the God of the Qur'an (29:46);
- God is 'appreciative' (a strange characteristic to attribute to an all-powerful God) of those who do good (42:23);
- God's kingship is associated with this world (13:2); and

- God invites everyone to heaven (10:25), which contrasts with Satan, who invites everyone to hell (35:6).

The final judgment continues to be a dominant theme in Muhammad's message as recorded in the Qur'an. In these third Meccan suras, the following statements stood out:

- it is possible to be so sinful that one is unredeemable (10:88-89, 90-91);
- heaven may not be eternal (11:108; 46:3);
- there will be arguing in hell (40:46-50);
- animals will be judged (6:38);
- the bad deeds of the righteous will be overlooked (46:16); and there is (at least a hint of) assurance for the righteous (7:35).
- Also, good deeds will count ten times to one's credit while a bad deed will count "with its equivalent" (6:160).

I also noted passages that are similar to Jesus' story about Lazarus and the rich man in Luke 16:19-31: those in hell are seen by those in paradise, and the believers in paradise are unable to give the requested reprieves to the punished (42:44-46; 7:50-51). In 7:163 we learn that God tempts the disbelieving people to break the Sabbath by causing fish to surface "only on [the Sabbath], never on weekdays" (7:163). Another similar type of action on God's part is mentioned in 6:42-45 where disbelievers are given prosperity by God, and

> "... as they revelled in what they had been given, we struck them suddenly and they were dumbfounded" (6:44).

(Parallel verses can be found in 7:94-96).

The only purpose I can think of for God needing to tempt people with fish or bring them prosperity before exacting judgment is that deeds in Islam have a weightier significance than mere belief or faith. If God can bring out their wickedness that shows their disbelief, He can, perhaps more justifiably, display his wrath. As a critique of this process of God bringing about his just wrath, - if suffering and affluence do not prove God's existence, as the unbelievers reasoned, "hardship and affluence also befell our forefathers" (7:95), then why is God's punishment in these cases just?

The third development I found in these third-period Meccan suras is in the way that Muhammad is portrayed. While he is still the warner he has maintained himself to be (46:9), it appears that he thought of himself as only sent to the Arabs (35:23-24), and not necessarily 'the seal of the prophets' that Muslims believe him to be today (the greatness of his prophethood, though, is more developed in the Medinan suras).

Another interesting feature is that on three occasions Muhammad claims that he had never heard of the stories that were revealed to him about Noah (11:49), Joseph (12:3, 102) and Moses (28:44) whose stories also occur in the Bible.

Reflections on the Suras from Medina
2, 98, 64, 62, 8, 47, 3, 61, 57, 4, 65, 59, 33, 63, 24, 58, 22, 48, 66, 60, 110, 49, 9, 5

The Medinan suras provide yet further distinction and development in the message as revealed to Muhammad. These can be summed up under three main categories:

- specific messages about current battles and fighting in the way of God;
- the development of Muhammad's message at the level of an initiation of a complete religion instead of a mere warning to turn away from polytheism;
- a further development in nature of the prophethood of Muhammad.

The Suras that mention battles include: sura 8 (battle of Badr), sura 47, sura 3 (battle of Badr and Uhud), sura 59, sura 33 (Battle of the Trench), sura 48, and sura 9 (preparations for the expeditions to Tabuk). Many interesting specific instructions are given in these Medinan suras:

- fighting during the fasting month is prohibited (2:217),
- but Muhammad leaves it ambiguous whether one can take part in killing when persecution is involved (2:217, cf. v.191);
- believers can "incur the wrath of God" in hell if they flee from a disbeliever while in battle (8:16);

- struggling for God's cause is listed as one ingredient for inheriting God's forgiveness (8:74);
- "fighting in God's way" involves killing other people (4:92-94) and is not merely an inner fight of oneself against sin as peaceful Muslims interpret *jihad*;
- there is a "high rank" and "tremendous reward" for those who take part in "striving in God's way" (4:95-96);
- from the context of 4:95, "striving in God's way" and "fighting in God's way" seem synonymous;
- while in battle, God does not protect those who pray—instructions are given to have some stand guard while others pray (4:101-103).

The development of Muhammad's revelations to include instructions about proper conduct and true worship in this period of revealed suras point to a shift in Muhammad's message from a mere warning against polytheism to the establishment of an identifiable, organized religion. Sura 2 particularly parallels Jesus' Sermon on the Mount (Mt. 5-8) and Moses' instructions on various procedures for the Israelites in Deuteronomy. Sura 2 speaks of the direction of prayer (v.142-149), fasting (v.183-187), fighting (v.190-194, 216-218), pilgrimage (v.196-203), suffering (v.214-215), gambling (v.219-220), orphans (v.220), marriage with disbelievers (v.221), menstruation (v.222), sex (v.223), taking oaths (v224-227), divorce (v.228-232), breastfeeding (v.233), widows (v.234), refugees (v.243), and giving (v.261-281). Similarly, in providing specific instruction about daily life, suras four and five also give instructions for proper living for believers. A second way that the Medinan suras develop Islam as a religion is that they focus more on who is a "true believer" and who is not, especially among the Jews and Christians (62:6, 3:75ff, 3:199-200).

A third development in the Medinan suras is in the progress of the prophethood of Muhammad and his connection with God as the object of people's faith and belief (for example, 9:61, 62, 63, 65, 71, 74, 80, 84, 86, 90, 91, 94, 99; 5:81, 92). We see here a clear shift away from Muhammad being merely one of the prophets, specifically, one sent to Arab people as mentioned in the third Meccan period suras 35:23-24. Muhammad orders his followers not to raise their voices above his or "your [good] deeds may be cancelled out" (49:2). He could have access to specific women who were related to him or his slaves, while other believers could not (33:50-52) ("lawful to you," a sexual permission?). Further, Muhammad "is more protective towards the believers than they are themselves" (33:6). His wives are the mothers of believes (33:6) and will receive a double reward (33:31) if they are "obedient to God and His Messenger and [do] good deeds" (33:31). Contributions of some may bring them closer to the prayers of Muhammad and thereby, to God's mercy (9:99). Muhammad is described not only as concerned for his people, but full of mercy (9:128), an attribute that makes one question its relevancy if God's mercy is really the only thing that should matter to the believers. Furthermore, "God and his messenger" may make decisions together which are to be undisputed (33:36).

Among the interesting verses in this section, which are too numerous to list here, I was surprised to read a prohibition against eating food sacrificed to idols as in 5:3. One of the critiques of Muhammad's reforms in Arab society is that he employed near syncretistic practices in order to win the masses. The *hajj*, for example, was a pagan practice from before his time. The worship around the *kaba* was another polytheistic practice. Yet some of Muhammad's revelations did strictly separate believers from polytheists, and the case mentioned in 5:3 is even more strict than the Christian teaching on this topic (1 Cor. 8:4,8). Another example of the Qur'an diverting from syncretistic practices is mentioned in M.A.S. Abdel Haleem's introduction to Chapter 58, where Muhammad instigates a prohibition against a pagan divorce practice.

Christian Attitudes to the Prophet Muhammad[1]

Mark Beaumont[2]

The significance of Bishop Kenneth Cragg's *Muhammad and the Christian, A Question of Response* published in 1984 is hard to overstate. Here was the first book length treatment of the status of the Prophet Muhammad by this leading English Anglican statesman who had become synonymous with sensitive Christian interaction with Islam. As Cragg [d. 2012] points out, Christian and secular authors have formed a picture of Muhammad as a man who came to rule in sincerity but in so doing lost his prophetic integrity, but this should be set aside for the new view that he was consistent all the way through his calling.

We Christians should take "the Qur'an in positive terms, both in its time and through the centuries as effectively revelatory" (ibid, p94-5). This acknowledgement can be spelled out in greater detail.

> We receive in the Qur'an a powerful and telling reinforcement of Christian conviction as to the reality and rule of God, the divine creation, the earth tenancy and investiture of man, the divine liability about Him, the intelligible trust of His signs, the interacting claims of worship and dominion, the solemn joy of sexuality, and the awe of our personal being as lived 'in the light of His countenance'. Whatever the reservations we still have to make, and allowing the fact that predicates about God differ within their agreements, we are not thereby deprived of a community of belief with the people of the Qur'an which is authentic in its content and urgent in its significance [p118].

---

[1] This article considers attitudes to the Prophet Muhammad commencing with Kenneth Cragg's 1984 *Muhammad and the Christian, A Question of Response* to the present. It is a condensed version of Beaumont's article, 'Christian Views of Muhammad since the Publication of Kenneth Cragg's *Muhammad and the Christian, A Question of Response* in 1984', *Transformation* 32, (2015), pp145-62.

[2] Dr Mark Beaumont is a Senior Lecturer in Islam and Mission, London School of Theology

Cragg's deeper concern is that the prophethood of Muhammad is in ultimate conflict with the self-sacrifice of Jesus. Firstly, Jesus spoke of being more than a prophet in Mt 11:9. This is the Messiah redeeming 'more than' educating, of the divine word suffering to save 'more than' commanding. Secondly, the Qur'anic belief in the perfectibility of humans by the "persuasion of political establishment" (p130) is challenged by the Gospel teaching that "we may well be farthest from God in the very pretence of obeying Him" (p133). Thirdly, Muslim understanding of the sovereignty of God has been that He is exempt from real engagement with creation and humanity. Law, guidance, exhortation and judgment in Islam have to become grace, incarnation, suffering love and redemption. "Islam broadly disavows these as unfitting to divine sovereignty. The Gospel lives by them" (p137).

Cragg's view of the prophethood of Muhammad has set the agenda for those Christians who have written about Muhammad subsequently. There has been a spectrum of opinion about the kind of revelation brought by Muhammad, ranging from skeptical rejection to believing endorsement.

Muhammad did not bring revelation from God
English Anglican Ida Glaser argues that Muhammad believed that he was promoting the same message as Jews and Christians through the Biblical accounts that he heard and used. In the early Meccan years his call to worship one God seemed to him to be the message that he was drawn to from listening to Jews and Christians. "He was getting the opportunity to hear God through the biblically based material that he evidently knew" (I. Glaser, "Thinking Biblically about Islam", in *Between Naivety and Hostility: Uncovering the best Christian responses to Islam in Britain,* (eds) S. Bell and C. Chapman, Authentic: Milton Keynes, 2011, pp14-34, 31). Glaser sees Muhammad taking sincerely wrong decisions and moving further away from the voice of God. "Muhammad does not seem to have made the link between sacrifice and forgiveness…As Muhammad developed political power, he also took on the role of administering judgment, moving towards the position where he saw it as the role of the believers even to kill unbelievers in some circumstances" (p32).

From the perspective of the Bible there can hardly be another revelation from God when his word has been fully declared in Christ. But "if we were to allow another revelation after Christ, this could not be it" (p33). The revelation that Jesus brought was that God's kingdom is established through his death on the cross to redeem humanity from their rebellion against his rule. On the contrary, the message that Muhammad brought was that God's kingdom is established by submission to Muhammad's rule. "We cannot follow both the way of Muhammad, who established Islamic rule in Arabia, and the way of Jesus, who went to the cross in Jerusalem. There is a choice to be made" (p34).

Muhammad was not a prophet in the Biblical sense, and Christians should not call him a prophet but rather a man who led people to God

Jacques Jomier [d. 2008], a French Dominican father who spent twenty years in Egypt, hesitates to compare Muhammad with prophets found in the Bible. "If Christians were to accept the prophecy of Muhammad in the strict sense they would have to go against everything they are told by the weightiest religious documents in their possession" (J. Jomier, *How to Understand Islam*, SCM: London, 1989, p141). Muhammad's basic message "grafted simplified biblical or para-biblical ideas on to an Arab stem" (ibid, p144). However, the additions and subtractions he made to the prophetic language he heard undermine the purity of the original version.

Jomier argues that Christians should bypass the discussion of the prophethood of Muhammad in favour of affirming his spiritual teaching. He offers an example of how to do this from his experience of representing the Catholic Church in dialogue with Muslims.

> During a meeting between Muslims and Christians at al-Azhar, in Cairo, in April 1978, the grand imam Sheikh al-Azhar told the partners in dialogue representing the Vatican…that no dialogue would be possible as long as Christians did not respect the person of Muhammad…I said to one of the Muslims in the official delegation…that Muhammad was a religious figure, an exceptional politician, a brilliant man. But if Christians respected Muhammad as Muslims do, they would become Muslims. 'How do you want us to respect him,' I asked, 'while remaining Christians?' The sheikh replied that he personally was not a Hindu, but that he had a great respect for Gandhi and admired his person and actions (p141).

Jomier holds that through Muhammad's teaching "many people have learned to pray and to worship God" (p144).

Muhammad is not a Prophet in the Biblical sense but Christians may refer to him as the Prophet of Islam

Chawkat Moucarry, raised as a Syrian Catholic but now a Protestant, believes that Muhammad thought he was following prophets named in the Bible so the Christian must compare his message with theirs. On the positive side, he preached the oneness of God in a polytheistic Arab context. "The Qur'an presents a coherent body of beliefs about God, creation, revelation, humankind, the general resurrection and the Day of judgment, to mention only the major themes...God's attributes in Islam broadly correspond to what we find in the Bible" (C. Moucarry, *Faith to Faith. Christianity & Islam in dialogue,* IVP: Leicester, 2001, p257). On the negative side, the Qur'an "fails to point to God as the *Saviour,* the God who achieved our salvation through the death and resurrection of Jesus Christ...Because the Qur'an does not know God in this way, it fails to recognize the very nature of Jesus' mission" (ibid).

Moucarry concludes that Muhammad's mission falls short from a Christian perspective, and Christians have no alternative "but to challenge his credentials as a prophet" (p264). He refers to Christians who have accepted that Muhammad was a prophet, but a prophet sent only to the Arabs. But he rejects this concession because "the Qur'an includes accepting that Muhammad was sent to all peoples" (p265). While the Prophet of Islam is not a prophet in the Biblical way "he was probably the most zealous Arab for God in his generation" (p268). His knowledge of the gospel was partial, but he did not mislead his people for personal gain. He believed that God had called him to be a prophet and that the Qur'an was given to him by God, so his prophethood must be restricted to that frame of reference, as the Prophet of Islam.

Muhammad brought revelation from God, which needs to be completed by revelation in Jesus Christ

Fouad Elias Accad (d. 1994) was raised in the Lebanese Greek Orthodox Church. He became an ordained Protestant pastor who witnessed to Muslims by using passages from the Qur'an and the Bible as demonstrated in his *Seven Muslim-Christian Principles.* He used Qur'anic and Biblical texts together because he believed that "Muhammad did *not* in any way intend for the Qur'an to be anti-Christ or an anti-Christian document... Because of the largely pro-Christian attitude in the Qur'an, it seems just as legitimate to use it in our witnessing as to use a pro-Christian quote from any other respected book or leader" (F.E. Accad, *Building Bridges. Christianity and Islam,* NavPress: Colorado Springs, 1997, p28).

Muhammad brought revelation to the Arabs who did not have the word of God in Arabic. "Muhammad saw himself as a 'warner' who was bringing the Qur'an in a clear Arabic tongue in order to fill this literary vacuum within the Arab religious culture and to help turn the Arabs from idolatry to worship of the one true God" (ibid, p37). Muhammad agreed with orthodox Christian beliefs rather than opposing them. "When he confronted Christians about having three gods, he was not attacking the idea of the Father, Son, and Holy Spirit in the Godhead. He was attacking the idea of God having a wife and then having a son by her" (p58).

Muhammad was a Prophet of God who brought a message about Jesus that differed from orthodox Christian belief

William Montgomery Watt (d. 2006), Scottish Anglican Islamologist, is well known for his argument that the attack on the Trinity in the Qur'an is not against an orthodox Christian formulation, but rather against a heterodox community. "The idea that Mary was one of the Trinity may have come from an obscure sect of Collyridians, heard of in Arabia more than two centuries before Muhammad" (W. M. Watt, *Muslim-Christian Encounters: Perceptions and Misperceptions,* Routledge: London, 1991, p23).

Nevertheless, he acknowledges that the Qur'an does undermine important Christian beliefs, such as the incarnation and the death and resurrection of Jesus Christ. "The Christian of today should not take this as a reason for denying that Muhammad was inspired by God. What is necessary, rather, is a reconsideration of the nature of prophethood" (ibid, p24). Muhammad cannot be held responsible for not knowing mainstream Christianity. Christians should see Muhammad as "a religious leader through whom God has worked, and that is tantamount to holding that he is in some sense a prophet. Such a view does not contradict any central Christian belief" (p148).

Muhammad and Jesus complement each other

German Lutheran Martin Bauschke sees Christianity and Islam as equally valid modes of revelation. "God wanted both religions as authentic ways to salvation. God revealed himself to both, Jesus and Muhammad!" (M. Bauschke, "A Christian View of Islam", in, *Islam and Inter-Faith Relations,* (eds) P. Schmidt-Leukel and L. Ridgeon, SCM: London, 2007, pp137-155, 148). The Bible and the Qur'an are also equally the word of God. "If Christianity and Islam are equal ways to God, then Jesus and Muhammad shall become the two younger brothers of Moses, and the Bible and the Qur'ān shall become the second and third testaments of God, added to the first testament, the Torah" (ibid, p149).

Bauschke calls for "a theological recognition of Muhammad as God's Prophet" (p152). He understands "the mission of Jesus and of Muhammad, the revelation of the Word of God as incarnation and as inlibration[3] as being *complementary*...Jesus and Muhammad are not doubles, but brothers with similarities and differences" (ibid). He takes the complementarity of Jesus' powerless death and Muhammad's powerful rule as indicative of God's use of two modes of revelation.

---

[3] Ed. note: *inlibration* is derived from *libro'* meaning book: i.e. "having been turned into a book" or inscripturation. Muslims believe that the Qur'an exists in a tablet in heaven and that it was revealed to Muhammad to be written down.

The Deaths of Jesus and Muhammad: Implications for Historicity

Anthony McRoy[1]

Introduction

It is unsurprising that we find little historical corroboration outside, respectively, Christian and Muslim sources, for the birth of either Jesus or Muhammad, simply because they were not the sons of Kings or nobles. What, however, about their deaths? The deaths of low-born figures such as ordinary politicians, rock stars, actors and such others are noted because of their renown *subsequent* to their birth. This paper will comparatively examine the data concerning the deaths of Jesus and Muhammad, and note the consequences for the historicity of their proponent religious literature.

Jesus

The consensus of primary sources is that Jesus was crucified under Pilate, Prefect (i.e. governor) of Judaea, so He must have been crucified A.D. 26–36. This is the common testimony of the New Testament.[2] Luke 3.1 refers to Jesus' forerunner, John the Baptist, commencing his ministry in 'the fifteenth year of the reign of Tiberius Caesar, when Pontius Pilate was governor of Judaea.', and 3.2 mentions 'Philip the Tetrarch', who died 34 A.D. Tiberius became Emperor in 14 A.D., so his fifteenth year would

> *The consensus of primary sources is that Jesus was crucified under Pilate, Prefect (i.e. governor) of Judaea, so He must have been crucified A.D. 26–36.*

---

[1] Dr McRoy, of dual UK/Eire nationality, is Lecturer in Islamic Studies at Union School of Theology in Wales, and author of and contributor to several books. He is married with three grown-up children.

[2] Mathew 27.2ff; Mark 15.1ff; Luke 3.1; 13.1; 23.1ff; John 18.28ff; 19.1ff; Acts 4.27; 1 Timothy 6.13.

have been c. 29 A.D. allowing for the Roman calendar. Coins issued by Pilate exist, dated from the sixteenth (c.28-29) to the eighteenth year of Tiberius (i.e. 31-32 A.D.), so it would seem that Luke's time-frame is accurate.[3]

The death of what Romans would doubtless regard as an insignificant religious fanatic and/or insurgent in a remote backwater would not have occasioned any *immediate* contemporary comment, but as the Christian movement grew, more attention would be devoted to it. The Jewish author Josephus, c. 93 A.D., states that Jesus was crucified by Pilate: 'Pilate, at the suggestion of the principal men amongst us, had condemned him to the cross.'[4] It is sometimes held that part or all of this passage has been interpolated by Christian apologists, but no manuscripts exist which excise any reference to Jesus' crucifixion, and Jerome (c. 340-420) rendered Josephus thus: 'He ... was believed to be Christ, and when through the envy of our chief men Pilate had crucified him.'[5] Likewise the Roman pagan writer Tacitus (c. 116), no friend of Christianity, states that Pilate ordered the execution of Jesus: 'Christus ... suffered the extreme penalty during the reign of Tiberius at the hands of one of our procurators, Pontius Pilatus.'[6]

There is no contrary evidence that Jesus was executed anytime outside the rule of Pilate, or that He died otherwise or disappeared. The threefold cord of early Jewish, pagan and Christian historical sources all agree that Jesus was indeed executed, and during the rule of Pontius Pilate, so no later than 36, and no earlier than 26 A.D.

Muhammad

The problem is that the Muslim sources for Muhammad's death are all late, e.g. the *Sirah of Ibn Ishaq*, referring to the author who died in 761 – that is, around 130 years after Muhammad's supposed death. It is well-known that his work only survives in part, specifically

> *The problem is that the Muslim sources for Muhammad's death are all late.*

---

[3] Madden, Frederic W., *Coins of the Jews*, London: Trübner & Company, 1881, pp.182-183.

[4] Josephus, *Antiquities of the Jews*, 18.2, 3.

[5] Jerome, *Lives of Illustrious Men,* Chapter XIII.

[6] Tacitus, *Annals* 15.44.

through the work of Ibn Hisham, who died c. 833, meaning that this work is even further removed from the actual events.

The *Sirah* states that the invasion of Palestine was led by Usama bin Zayd, rather than Muhammad himself:

The Sending of Usama B. Zayd to Palestine
Then the apostle returned and stopped in Medina. He ordered the people to make an expedition to Syria and put over them Usama b. Zayd b: Harith. He ordered him to lead his cavalry into Palestine.[7]

Immediately after this, we read how Muhammad's fatal illness began:

The Beginning of the Apostle's Illness
... the apostle began to suffer from the illness by which God took him to what honour and compassion He intended for him shortly before the end of Safar or in the beginning of Rabiul-awwal. It began, so I have been told, when he went to Baqiul-Gharqad in the middle of the night and prayed for the dead. Then he returned to his family and in the morning his sufferings began. Then it was that the illness through which God took him began.

Yaqub b. Utba from Muhammad b. Muslim al-Zuhri from Ubaydullah b. Abdullah b. Utba b. Masud from Aisha, the prophet's wife, said: The apostle returned from the cemetery to find me suffering from a severe headache and I was saying, 'O my head!' He said, 'Nay, Aisha, O my head!' Then he said, 'Would it distress you if you were to die before me so that I might wrap you in your shroud and pray over you and bury you?' Then his pain overcame him as he was going the round of his wives, until he was overpowered in the house of Maymuna.[8]

---

[7] Guillaume, A. *The Life of Muhammad: A Translation of Ishaq's Sirat Rasul Allah*, Oxford and Karachi: Oxford University Press, 1955, 1967, 2004, p678.

[8] Guillaume, p678.

The origins of this purportedly go back to when Muhammad conquered Khaybar, a supposedly Jewish stronghold in Arabia, and a Jewess gave him poisoned lamb:

The Rest of the Affair of Khaybar
When the apostle had rested Zaynab d. al-Harith, the wife of Sallam b. Mishkam prepared for him a roast lamb, having first inquired what joint he preferred. When she learned that it was the shoulder she put a lot of poison in it and poisoned the whole lamb. Then she brought it in and placed it before him. He took hold of the shoulder and chewed a morsel of it, but he did not swallow it. The apostle spat it out, saying, 'This bone tells me that it is poisoned.' Then he called for the woman and she confessed, and when he asked her what had induced her to do this she answered: 'You know what you have done to my people. I said to myself, If he is a king I shall ease myself of him and if he is a prophet he will be informed (of what I have done).' So the apostle let her off.

Marwan b. Uthman b. Abu Sa'id b. al-Mu'alla told me: The apostle had said in his illness of which he was to die when Umm Bishr d. al-Bara' came to visit him, 'O Umm Bishr, this is the time in which I feel a deadly pain from what I ate ... at Khaybar. The Muslims considered that the apostle died as a martyr in addition to the prophetic office with which God had honoured him.[9]

In terms of his actual death, the *Sirah* does not actually present a date:

The Apostle's Illness in the House of Aisha
The apostle died with the heat of noon that day. Al-Zuhri said that Anas b.Malik told him that on the Monday ... on which God took His apostle he went out to the people as they were praying the morning prayer.[10]

It would seem from this that Muhammad died on a Monday, subsequent to the Khaybar conquest and also the invasion of

---

[9] Guillaume, p516.

[10] Guillaume, p679.

Palestine. Usually, the first raids are dated to 629, with the conquest of Palestine in 634-40. Typically, Muhammad's death is dated to 632. The *Hadith,* compiled two centuries after Muhammad, agrees that he died on a Monday, the result of the poisoning at Khaybar:

> Narrated by Anas ibn Malik
> Sahih Al-Bukhari 1.648
> AbuBakr used to lead the people in prayer during the fatal illness of the Prophet. ... till it was Monday. When the people aligned (in rows) for the prayer the Prophet lifted the curtain of his house and started looking at us and was standing at that time. On the same day he died."

> Narrated by Aisha
> Sahih Al-Bukhari 5.713A
> The Prophet during his illness from which he died, used to say, "O Aisha! I still feel the pain caused by the food I ate at Khaybar, and at this time, I feel as if my aorta is being cut by that poison."

> Narrated by Umm Mubashshir
> Abu Dawud 4499
> Umm Mubashshir said to the Prophet ... during the sickness of which he died: What do you think about your illness, Apostle of Allah? I do not think about the illness of my son except the poisoned sheep of which he had eaten with you at Khaybar. The Prophet ... said: And I do not think about my illness except that. This is the time when it cut off my aorta.

These texts give Muhammad the dignity of a martyr, poisoned by a Jewess, of which people the Qur'an presents as the objects of Allah's anger (Surah Fatiha 1.7) and the most hostile to Muslims (Surah Maidah 5.82).

The first problem is that *external* sources do *not* corroborate the Muslim sources, and the second is that these sources are earlier, even contemporary and thus, historically, to be preferred. Our third problem is that unlike with the death of Jesus, Muhammad by the time of his death was an important political leader, and Palestine had been transformed into a vital part of the Byzantine Empire by virtue of Christian pilgrimage to its prestigious holy sites. His death would indeed be noted.

The *Doctrina Jacobi,* dated 634, by a Jew who had been forcibly baptised, indicates that Muhammad was still alive then:

When [Sergius] the *candidatus* was killed by the Saracens[11] we Jews were overjoyed. And they were saying, "A prophet has appeared, coming with the Saracens and he is preaching the arrival of the anointed one who is to come, the Messiah." And when I arrived in Sykamina, I visited an old man who was learned in the scriptures, and I said to him, "What can you tell me about the prophet who has appeared with the Saracens?" And he said to me, groaning loudly, "He is false, for prophets do not come with a sword and a war-chariot."[12]

The Secrets of Rabbi Simon ben Yohai, dated 635-45 also indicates that Muhammad was still alive at the time of its composition:

> ... Metatron, the foremost angel ... answered him and said: "Do not fear. for the Almighty only brings the kingdom of Ishmael in order to deliver you from this wicked one (Edom). He raises up over them (Ishmaelites) a prophet according to His will."[13]

The Nestorian *Khuzistan Chronicle* (c. 660) also seems to imply that Muhammad was alive when the Arabs invaded Persia and the Levant:[14]

> Then God raised up against them the sons of Ishmael ... whose leader ... was Muhammad ... they gained control over the entire land of the Persians. They also came to Byzantine territory, plundering and ravaging the entire region of Syria. Heraclius, the Byzantine king, sent armies against them, but the Arabs killed more than 100,000 of them.[15]

---

[11] Ed Note: The term *Saracens* came to be used to identify the people living in the area of Saudi Arabia and by implication was applied to Muslims living in that area. It would seem that the term was first used by Ptolemy in 2nd century CE.

[12] Shoemaker, Stephen J, *The Death of a Prophet: The End of Muhammad's Life and the Beginning of Islam*, Philadelphia: University of Pennsylvania Press, 2012, p2 2.

[13] Hoyland, Robert G., *Seeing Islam as Others Saw It: A Survey and Evaluation of Christian, Jewish and Zoroastrian Writings on Early Islam*, Princeton: Darwin Press, 199, p309.

[14] Ed Note: The Levant is a term that is used to primarily describe those lands adjoining the eastern shores of the Mediterranean Sea. In current terms it refers to the following countries: Cyprus, Israel, Jordan, Lebanon, Palestine, and Syria.

[15] Hoyland., p186.

At the other end of the Christological spectrum, the Miaphysite Chronological Charts (691-92) of Jacob of Edessa misdate the death of Muhammad to c. 627, but also misdate the raids into Palestine to 625-26, again indicating that Muhammad was alive during the attack on Palestine.[16] Shoemaker also notes several other sources from 717 onwards which suggest that Muhammad was alive during the Palestine invasion. There is also an alleged letter from Caliph 'Umar II (717-20) to Byzantine Emperor Leo II (717-41) dated late eighth century where 'Umar declares in relation to Muhammad's commission to *jihad* that 'with him in whom we trust, and in him in whom we believe, we went off ... to fight Persia and Byzantium.'[17]

> ... because the later Muslim sources state Muhammad was dead, these non-Muslim sources must err.

Hence, the external sources (and one Muslim source) suggest that Muhammad was still alive past 632. It might be argued that these sources are confused, but this depends upon anachronism and theological prejudice; that is, because the later Muslim sources state Muhammad was dead, these non-Muslim sources must err. The other problem is that non-Muslim sources are closer in time to the events they depict than the *Sirah* and *Hadith*. Ehrman, a liberal Biblical scholar favoured by Islamic polemicists, makes this very valid point: 'Historians prefer to have sources that are relatively near the date of the person or event that they are describing.'[18] Hence, according to the earliest sources, Muhammad did *not* die in 632.

Why the discrepancy? Shoemaker suggests local Yathribi[19] parochialism and that the emerging cult of Yathrib as the 'city of the Prophet' tied to Abbasid denigration of the Jerusalem-centric Marwanids produced a new tradition of Muhammad's martyrdom in Yathrib, allowing for his mosque to become an alternative centre

---

[16] Shoemaker, *The Death of a Prophet*, p37.

[17] Shoemaker, p59ff; Hoyland, p490ff.

[18] Ehrman, Bart D., *Did Jesus Exist?: The Historical Argument for Jesus of Nazareth*, New York: Harper Collins, 2012, p41.

[19] Yathrib is also known as Medina.

of pilgrimage and devotion rather than the Temple Mount.[20] This may be possible, if one accepts the premise that Jerusalem under the Marwanids was meant to be the premier focus of pilgrimage.

Another possibility concerns deteriorating relations between Jews and Muslims. The earliest sources do not depict any Jewish-Muslim controversy; in fact, Jews were doubtless overjoyed that persecuting Byzantines were vanquished (as the *Doctrina Jacobi* indicates), and probably hoped that they would be allowed to rebuild their Temple. However, the Arab conquerors sequestered the Mount for themselves, and under the Marwanids, intensified their presence therein. It is probably from this time that harsh attitudes towards the Jews began, culminating in antagonistic Hadiths about the Muslims fighting the Jews before the Hour.

The reason to fight the Byzantines and Persians was that they were politically empowered, but this was not true of the Jews. What better way for the Caliphate to justify hostility than to borrow from the smear against 'Jews as Christ-killers' to accuse them of being 'Messenger-killers'? This could be tied to the Jewish claim to the Mount:

> Narrated by Aisha
> Sahih Al-Bukhari 2.414
> The Prophet ... in his fatal illness said, Allah cursed the Jews and the Christians because they took the graves of their Prophets as places for worship".

His death by poisoning would also elevate Muhammad to the level of a martyr – rather like Jesus, commemorated by Jerusalem's Holy Sepulchre.

Summary

The external corroboration for the death of Jesus under Pontius Pilate is early and diverse enough (i.e. Jewish and pagan sources) to render acceptance of its historicity unassailable by objective analysis. That tends to support claims of historicity concerning the New Testament presentation of His life. The same cannot be said regarding the death of Muhammad. External sources in this case indicate that he was still alive after 632, when Muslim sources indicate that he died. Moreover, the external sources – in a

---

[20] Shoemaker, *The Death of a Prophet*, pp258-258.

reverse of the evidence concerning Jesus – have historical priority, whereas Muslim sources are very late. If Islamic traditions about Muhammad's death are historically questionable, what does that say about the historical reliability of the Islamic sources (*Sirah* and *Hadith*) in general?

Communiques

Evaluating a Local Church's Ministry to Muslims

"A critical analysis of the evangelistic activity carried out by an Inner City Church amongst Muslims resident in a Government Housing Estate from 1995 to 2015".

William Anderson[1]

Synopsis

Evangelism amongst Muslims typically meets with very limited outward success. This report critically examines the work done by an inner city Australian church, that has been engaging with Muslims on a nearby high-rise government housing estate. It analyses the outcomes achieved and issues faced, and assesses possible future directions. It suggests that the ministry is mostly moving in the right direction; it is just that 'ploughing the ground' is hard. Improvements lie in better understanding of the issues faced by Muslims who might consider becoming Christians, some ways of navigating that; in better training, briefing and debriefing of workers by the leadership team, and in renewed prayer and vision. A shift in focus toward second-generation adult migrants may be worth considering.

Introduction

It is well known that ministry among Muslims has rarely seen much fruit. But even with more recent glimmers of hope,[2] outward evidence of 'success' has often been difficult to detect. This is the case with a ministry that an inner city church, in a major Australian city, has carried out on a nearby high-rise government housing estate. For decades, 1995-2015, caring and evangelistic activities have been carried out on these Estates. In the last 20 years

---

[1] William Anderson (a pseudonym) a migrant to this country, has spent time overseas working amongst Muslims. He is loving postgraduate studies at MST.

[2] A turning of the tide has been documented in many places, including David Garrison, *A Wind in the House of Islam*, Monument: WIGtake Resources, 2014.

this has included ministry to Muslim refugees who have settled there and despite considerable engagement with these people there has been very little observable 'fruit'. This report critically analyses this ministry by looking first at what has been done, and then at outcomes that have been observed. An analysis of the key issues faced is undertaken, with a special focus on the insights given by an understanding of the history and institutions of Islam, and an assessment given of the strengths and weaknesses of the ministry so far, followed by suggestions for 'best practice' as the ministry moves on.

Research Methodology

Aside from the usual documentary research, this report draws on the insights and experiences of a number of people interviewed by its author. Interviews were mostly carried out by telephone or in person, and recorded as audio files. In most cases, interviewees were sent a basic set of questions beforehand by email. Limited in number, these interviews are not statistically or otherwise analysed, rather they are used as material to stimulate and supplement the insights and experiences of the author as he reflects on the ministry being carried out among Muslims. The author has also been in charge of the ministry in recent years, and draws on his own insights and experiences.

The Housing Estates

The high-rise buildings that currently constitute the bulk of the housing estate under study were built in the 1960s. Current redevelopment, a mixture of public and private housing, is occurring over some parts of the estate. The public housing communities in these new developments are very similar to those in the existing buildings.

People living on these estates have primarily been refugee immigrants. Waves of refugees from different parts of the world have arrived at different times. Workers in the eighties report a predominance of Southern Europeans.[3] Workers in the nineties report a significant Asian influx, particularly Vietnamese and

---

[3] Elizabeth (pseudonym), pers. comm., 2013.

Chinese.[4] Then some twenty years ago, a new wave of immigrants started arriving, refugees from the Horn of Africa; who, unlike other migrants, have mostly stayed on the Estates, and are raising families there. A snapshot of the current Estates community reflecting tenant records[5] is given below.

A snapshot of the character of the current Estates community

The double 'bump' reflects the number of families having children (p59). There are also significant numbers of older people; often these are migrants from previous generations still in public housing. Australia is by far the largest country by birth; which is accounted for by the majority of children having been born here[6]. Other birth demographics and preferred languages again show the predominance of Horn of African peoples, particularly Somalis. The large number of people preferring English as a communication language shows the settled nature of the migrant population, most having lived here many years.

Age Group	Number
0 - 5 Years	179
6 - 15 Years	340
15 - 18 Years	75
18 - 24 Years	99
25 - 55 Years	601
55 - 75 Years	315
Over 75 Years	106
Grand Total	**1715**

Workers interviewed for this report mentioned interacting with Turkish, Lebanese[7], Somali, Ethiopian and Eritrean Muslims in the early period. Currently the most noticeable group are the Somalis. According to one worker[8], they are predominantly from one area (Puntland)[9]; but other major groups are Eritrean Muslims, and Oromo and Harari Muslims from Ethiopia. Turkish and Lebanese populations have declined and a few Iraqi Shi'ite

---

[4] Sean, phone interview by the author (21st May, 2015). Interviewee name a pseudonym. Many other church members from that era have reported this.

[5] There are known to be additional unofficial tenants living with Estate residents. While accurate, the source of these figures does not wish to be identified.

[6] The author also knows of Australian born adult residents on the Estates. These are few in number.

[7] This includes some Lebanese Druze, whom many Muslims consider not to be Muslim.

[8] Chris, phone interview by the author (13th May, 2015). Interviewee name a pseudonym.

[9] There are some from the Somali part of Ethiopia (Ogaden), and a few from other places.

Muslims have arrived. There is at least one Western convert to Islam.

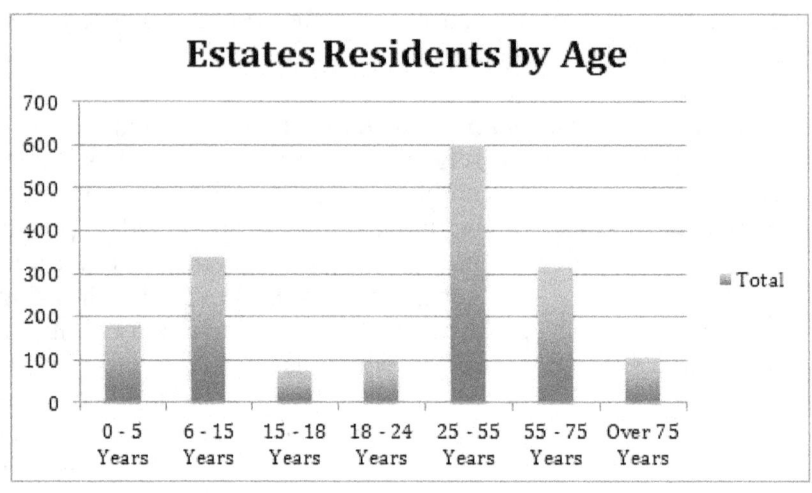

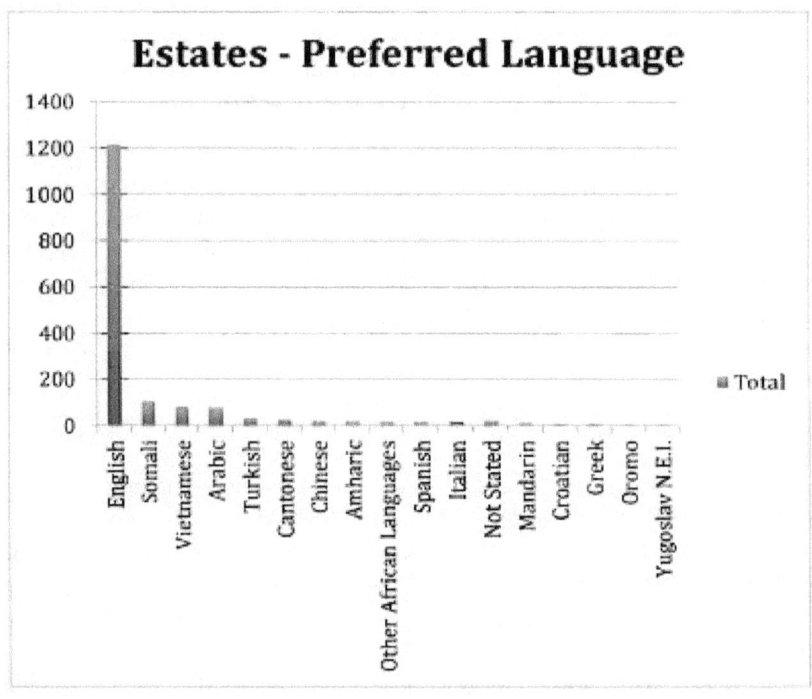

Country of Birth	Total	Country of Birth	Total
Australia	725	Italy	24
Somalia	208	Southern Europe	20
Ethiopia	93	Chile	15
Vietnam	90	Lebanon	15
Eritrea	64	New Zealand	15
China	63	Kenya	14
Sub-Saharan Africa	63	Hong Kong (SAR of China)	12
Turkey	42	Greece	10
Egypt	39	Iraq	10
Sudan	28	All Other Countries	135
Not Stated	30	**Grand Total**	1715

Preferred Language	Total	Preferred Language	Total
English	1211	Oromo	6
Somali	105	Yugoslav N.E.I.	6
Vietnamese	80	Burmese	5
Arabic	78	Portuguese	4
Turkish	33	Swahili	4
Cantonese	29	Afrikaans	3
Chinese	21	Tigrinya	3
Amharic	18	Maltese	2
Other African Languages	17	Bulgarian	1
Spanish	17	Hungarian	1
Italian	16	Macedonian	1
Not Stated	22	Other Asian Languages	1
Mandarin	12	Polish	1
Croatian	8	Russian	1
Greek	8	Slovenian	1
		Grand Total	1715

Activities carried out amongst Muslims on the estates by the church in 1995-2015

The church under study has carried out various caring ministries over the last twenty years for Muslims and non-Muslims alike. These have included holiday camps[10]; picnics and other day outings; and tutoring, either in a formal setting such as a weekly homework club or TESOL class, or informally in people's homes. Home tutoring has often evolved into friendships where all sorts of practical help is given to families in navigating Western society.

The church has also provided material support from a locally situated workshop, from which household items are recycled, fabricated and repaired. The workshop manager has been a particularly long-term worker on the estates. He is greatly trusted and appreciated by the residents.[11] Donations of furniture, and gifts to give away at Christmas, are received from churches in wealthier suburbs.

In the past a breakfast club was run at a nearby school, and food distributed. Community lunches have been run in association with a Sunday service and Sunday School. A weekly Kids Club has provided a social outlet for primary aged children over the whole period. Annual Easter and Christmas festival events have been run. Youth group events have run, also adult Bible study groups in homes and aged care groups in community spaces. Women's weekends away have been organised and a twice-weekly sewing group has run for more than a decade. Recently youth soccer competitions (in cooperation with a local YMCA) have been organised as well as a midnight Ramadan soccer program. Relationships developed through all these activities have often led to church members visiting homes or being part of family and other celebrations. Prayer groups, paid staff, organising committees and training activities have supported these programs.

---

[10] Families have been taken on five-day subsidised trips to beachside campsites.

[11] A letter written to the Housing Manager by two Muslim men in 2014 says this about the person concerned (a church employee), "[He] has gained the trust of all the housing estate residents from all ages and backgrounds or religions. Families, young, pensioners whenever they need help, [he] is available for them anytime. Women in particular trust [him], just meet anyone on the estates or knock on any door. Refugees and people who move to the estates, most of them don't have furniture, they come to the local workshop and ask for [him]..."

How were Muslims exposed to the Gospel, and how was it commended to them? What responses were observed?

Muslims started arriving on the Estates in the mid-nineties, but were low in number.[12] A volunteer worker remarked that much of the interaction between church workers and the new arrivals was "needs based"; new arrivals needed to find their way, and the church helped them.[13] However as volunteers helped with various needs, relationships were established, and in this context Christian faith was on display and was discussed.[14] All workers said this was the main way the Gospel was shared and commended, which has continued into the present.

The Gospel message has also been expressed in more formal settings, so in the early 2000s, Somali, Turkish and other Muslims came to the Sunday community lunch and stayed on for the service.[15] At family camps and at Christian festival events Muslims were (of their own volition) exposed to Christian community, teaching and worship.[16] Over the years, hundreds of Christian tracts, Jesus DVDs and Bibles in various languages have also been distributed. Workers have worked hard at presenting the Gospel in contextual ways.[17]

When asked about 'success stories', the following came to light. Several interviewees mentioned an elderly Turkish lady. She came to Sunday services even though her English was very limited and was befriended. She liked the music, and was given Christian

---

[12] Sean, phone interview by the author (21st May, 2015). Sean was Minister in charge of this ministry from 1993-1998. The dominant group and main ministry focus on the estates at that time were the Vietnamese.

[13] Chris. This needs-based activity has declined, and Chris would prefer we shift our energy onto second-generation young adults.

[14] Sean reported an example of this. An Eritrean Muslim teenager started attending the youth group and participating in Bible studies. He had no intention of becoming a Christian; rather he liked the atmosphere in the group and wanted to learn more about Australian culture.

[15] Peter, phone interview by the author (19th May, 2015). Interviewee name a pseudonym. Peter was Minister in charge of this ministry from 1999-2011.

[16] So for example, Muslim families chose to participate in Christmas plays and listened into the devotional times after breakfast at camp.

[17] Sarah, phone interview by the author (20th May, 2015). Interviewee name used is a pseudonym. So for example, Sarah said she would often talk about what it felt like to have a personal relationship with God, how it changed the way she lived, and so on.

Turkish materials, a Bible and a Jesus DVD. Eventually she had to leave the estates and has since died. Before her death, however, a Christian Turkish speaker spent some time with her and was convinced she was genuinely converted.[18]

A young Somali woman seriously contemplated becoming a Christian. She was particularly close to one worker and had been a regular at activities put on by the church. However, when confronted with the consequences of conversion, she backed away. In the words of her friend, "… to be Somali was to be Muslim; it was part of their [sic] identity; she had no models for how she could be Somali and Christian."[19] In the end none of the workers spoken to had any confidence that this girl had become even a hidden believer, even though she had been very close to accepting Christ.

Several volunteer workers became very close to particular families, and were even accepted as family by those families.[20] The author has also heard three or four accounts of different Muslims saying to workers something along the lines of 'whenever we need help, it is always you Christians who help us, not the [sic] Muslims'![21] While not necessarily evangelistic 'success', workers commented it was hard to know exactly what went on internally for some of their Muslim friends.

Negative responses to the church activities have also been experienced. At one family fun day, the author spoke about a parable of Jesus. Immediately a Somali woman stood up and loudly proclaimed that God hadn't had sex with Mary, that He had no children, that there was only one God, and that His name was

---

[18] Peter, interview; also Amy, phone interview by the author (19th May, 2015); Karen, phone interview by the author (20th May, 2015). Interviewee names are pseudonyms.

[19] Her friend had met Somali Christians in other places, however all the stories she knew had been of converts having to give up family, community and identity, which this girl could not bring herself to do.

[20] For example, one collected a 'dowry' of household items for a volunteer worker who was getting married; another went on holidays with a worker family. Karen; phone interview by the author. Linda, phone interview by the author (17th May, 2015). Interviewee names are pseudonyms. An extraordinary healing after a worker prayed for her great impacted a Muslim woman. Amy, phone interview by the author

[21] Two of these comments were directed at him personally.

Allah.[22] At a recent festival on the estates a Somali Muslim was incensed to see Somali Bibles amongst Bibles in several other languages on a literature stand. Following that, another Somali sent an email to the author and various other government and community agencies, accusing the church of various things, but particularly of trying to convert Muslims to Christianity, which the writer asserted was 'unethical'.

Key Issues faced by the Church's Evangelistic Activity amongst Muslims on the Estates

The lack of visible response is a key issue for ministry on the estates. There are many factors contributing to this: firstly, strong cultural and religious barriers that work against Muslims becoming Christians; secondly, questions as to how clearly the Gospel is being articulated, and thirdly, questions as to how well workers are being equipped and encouraged. For the sake of brevity, this report will now focus on the main group of Muslims currently on the estates, namely the Somalis.[23]

It is very apparent that the main factor working against Somalis becoming Christians is the strong identification they have with being Muslim.[24] This strong identification is influenced by both culture and religion; one feeds off the other. Somali culture has its roots in a nomadic, clan-based existence. Group identity and group pressure remain culturally strong[25] and breaking with the group is greatly to be feared.[26] In a land where pastures are few, Somalis had to be assertive and strong. Even now they consider

---

[22] This seemed to the author mostly an honour-shame reaction; she was upholding the honour of Islam after I had upheld the honour of the Christian faith.

[23] The other Muslim groups yield similar concerns, but perhaps not as strongly.

[24] So for example, the woman at the centre of the film, 'I Against My Brother', says: "I am a Somali Christian, a contradiction", since to be Somali is to be Muslim. -, -, 'I Against My Brother' in *Somalistory*. http://somalistory.com (Accessed 29 May, 2015).

[25] Yakim, email interview by the author (19th May, 2015). Interviewee name is a pseudonym.

[26] "One of the greatest fears for a Somali is to become "idla" – without a people or family group.", 'The Somali People – Year of Prayer Guide' in *Somalistory*. http://prayforsomalia.org/Library/booklets/YOPS_english.pdf (30 January, 2008), 8.

themselves a warrior people.[27] Islam reinforced these things. There is in Islam the strong expectation that Islam will rule the world,[28] and that Muslims are 'the best of people'.[29] Somali history has also played into this; Islam came to Somalia as early as the seventh century; by the tenth century the Arab settlement of Mogadishu was bringing wealth and influence; and by 1100 AD most Somalis had converted. They then fought holy Wars against the Ethiopian Christians, and became dominant in the land.[30] Islam gave Somalis a distinctive from surrounding peoples. Similarly, fear of breaking with the group has joined with the strong religious censor that exists for leaving Islam. Apostasy is viewed as deserving death in the Qur'an[31] and in the hadith[32]; there is a strong sense that leaving Islam is the ultimate group betrayal.[33] This is compounded with a strong fear that if you turn away from Islam, God will punish you.[34] An outworking of all this on the estates is a lot of religious 'policing' in the Somali community; so what is said and done in public spaces is often very different to what happens behind closed doors.[35]

---

[27] 'Where do they come from?' in *The Somalis of London – posted by Somalis for Jesus*. https://www.facebook.com/pages/SOMALI-CHRISTIANS/109046185783592 (Accessed 20 May, 2015).

[28] So in the Qur'an: Allah "has sent His Messenger with guidance and the religion of truth (Islam), to make it superior [or prevail] over all religions even though the Mushrikin (non-Muslims) hate (it). (Q. 9:33; 48:28; 61:9). All Qur'anic quotations are taken from Muhammad Taqi-ud-Din Al-Hilali (trans.) and Muhammad Muhsin Khan (trans.) *The Noble Qur'an: English Translation of the Meanings and Commentary* (Medina: King Fahd Complex for the Printing of the Holy Qur'an, n.d.).

[29] A phrase borrowed from the Qur'an: "You are the best of peoples evolved for mankind, enjoining what is right, forbidding what is wrong, and believing in Allah." (Q.3:110).

[30] Ann H. S Hurgin, 'Somalia' in *Countries and Their Cultures* http://www.everyculture.com/Sa-Th/Somalia.html (Accessed 21 May 2015)

[31] "... But if they turn back (from Islam), take (hold of) them and kill them wherever you find them, and take neither *Auliya* (protectors or friends) nor helpers from them." (Q.4.89).

[32] Bukhari, volume 9, book 84, hadith 57, records Muhammad's statement that, "Whoever changed his [Islamic] religion, then kill him", quoted in Patrick Sookhdeo, *Freedom to Believe* (McLean: Isaac Publishing, 2009) 23.

[33] The average Somali estates resident may know little of the Qur'an, but this worldview is clearly present in his thinking.

[34] Many workers noted that their conversations with Somalis evidenced these themes.

[35] Several workers noted this, and there are many examples. One may suffice: every year huge numbers of Christmas presents have been given away to Somalis, but last year when a religious authority in Somalia issued a ban on any sort of participation in Christmas, no Somali came to get a Christmas present.

Islamic worldviews also contribute to a strong distrust of Christianity,[36] present in this locality, too, so there is a strong belief in the logic of the Muslim faith and the illogicality of the Christian faith.[37]

It is difficult to account for the clarity with which the Gospel is being presented as most evangelistic activity occurs on the estates in the context of personal relationships. Volunteer workers naturally shy away from conflict. Misunderstandings possibly arise as Islamic worldviews tend to interpret Christians kindness as an effort to be good people, subconsciously reinforcing the idea that Christians have the same understanding of salvation as Muslims do.[38] To counteract this the previous Minister in charge of ministry on the estates put a lot of work into training volunteer workers on the estates. He regularly met to brief and debrief them, often one to one.[39] This is a very helpful strategy, and although continued by the author, has declined in strength. The team also historically spent much time in prayer; this too has declined recently as other ministries have detracted somewhat from an estates focus. Little visible success has at times also contributed a reduction in team numbers.

Ministry Strengths and Weaknesses; and Ways Forward for the Future

Looking at what workers elsewhere are reporting,[40] and reading many accounts of Somalis who have become Christians, indicates that much of the ministry on the estates is moving in the right direction. Everywhere barriers to conversion mean little visible fruit. However, Somalis are becoming Christians and relationships have been key in this; if not before conversion, then

---

[36] Workers amongst Somalis in East Africa report 'propaganda' about Christians and Christian teaching as a major barrier to hearing the Gospel. Stephen Thompson, email interview by the author (19th May, 2015). Interviewee name used with permission; Keith, email interview by the author (28th May, 2015). Interviewee name is a pseudonym.

[37] A viewpoint reinforced in the Qur'an, e.g. "Say (O Muhammad): "He is Allah, (the) One... He begets not, nor was he begotten." (Q.113:1,3). Even though Somali Muslims typically don't know the Qur'an, its worldview seeps into the culture.

[38] These issues were mentioned by several respondents and have been part of the author's own experience.

[39] Peter; Karen.

[40] Julio Quirino, email interview by the author (26th May, 2015). Interviewee name used by permission.

soon after.⁴¹ Also, workers on the estates have generally been very aware of the need to talk about faith issues one-to-one with Somalis and some have done this boldly, wisely and well; without compromising the Gospel.

An improvement may lie in better understanding of 'the exit' issues for Somalis who leave Islam.⁴² Somali believers all over the world are in touch with each other via the Internet.⁴³ They are investigating Christianity via the Internet forums (e.g. PalTalk), and websites (e.g. somalichristians.org) and in this way communicating with other Somali believers.⁴⁴ Apparently there are Somali Christians in our major city in Australia, but they remain hidden.⁴⁵

Another improvement would be a greater focus on encouragement, training, briefing and debriefing. There is such a wealth of material now available to encourage workers and better contextualise the message.⁴⁶ The focus would be on scratching where Somalis are itching, as shown in various conversion stories.⁴⁷

---

⁴¹ So 'Bishar' in 'From Islamist militant to soldier of the cross', *Barnabas Aid* (Nov./Dec. 2013), 11, was converted as he read a magazine, but he needed to find a Christian fellowship in order to move on from there.

⁴² Yakim reports of a Somali girl in Sydney who became a believer but then distanced herself from the woman who had brought her the Gospel. She didn't tell her she had come to faith. They only found out by chance through an intermediary who was at a church the girl started going to. The girl explained she couldn't say anything because Yakim and the woman were too close to the Somali community. They 'knew her aunts'.

⁴³ Yakim.

⁴⁴ Craig, (pseudonym) Somali Christian Ministries, pers. comm. by email (14ᵗʰ May, 2015).

⁴⁵ This from a number of workers, including Yakim, Peter and Sarah. Yakim says, "I've talked to a trusted Somali believer in Kenya who told me about a number of believers in [3 major Australian cities]. All these connections are through the Somali 'e-church'. God is primarily using Somali believers to reach Somalis. In our city in the Horn, we know there's a handful of believers, but we have no clue who they are - and we're told that's for the better. The believers who we do know said to us: live holy lives - that will encourage the believer because they observe you (!), and it will prepare the ground for THEIR sharing by showing Christianity as an honourable faith".

⁴⁶ See in particular these websites and books: *Somalistory*. http://somalistory.com (Accessed 29 May, 2015); *Somali Christian Ministries*. http://somalichristians.org (Accessed 29 May, 2015); Ahmed Ali Haile, *Teatime in Mogadishu: My journey as a peace ambassador in the world of Islam* (Harrisonburg: Herald Press, 2011).

⁴⁷ Haile's book in particular gives good connections between Gospel and Somali culture, and pertinent ways of deflecting common Somali objections to the Christian faith. Other books just give good stories to tell Somalis. One the author likes is in Garrison, *A Wind in*

There is also good material that can carefully be used to point Somalis to websites where they can privately hear stories and the Gospel message.[48] Encouragement and training of workers would also seek renewed vision and prayer.

A final improvement might be to shift our focus to the second-generation young adults that we know. Australian-raised, but having to bridge two cultures; these people may be easier to engage with Gospel issues[49].

Conclusion
In critically analysing the evangelistic activity carried out by the church under study amongst Muslims resident on a housing estate from 1995 to 2015, it has been suggested that much of the ministry is moving in the right direction. Improvements lie in better understanding of issues for Muslims who might consider becoming Christians, in greater encouragement, training, briefing and debriefing of workers by the leadership team, and in renewed prayer and vision. A shift in focus toward second-generation adult migrants may be worth considering.

---

the House of Islam, 80-81. A Somali sheikh becomes a Christian and says, "you need to know that inside we are empty. Don't be afraid of us. We need the Gospel."

[48] *Somalistory, Somali Christian Ministries, Somalis for Jesus*
http://somalisforjesus.blogspot.com.au (Accessed 29 May, 2015).

[49] As suggested by the former volunteer worker, Chris. However, this would have to be done very discretely, and with trusted individuals!

Magdalena:
The use of film to target Muslim women

Rebecca Hayman[1]

Introduction
Most, if not all, Muslim societies have a predominantly shame/honour worldview and this one fact has been credited as a major reason for the West's apparent failure to communicate the Gospel to Muslims.[2] With this in mind, the title of the film *Magdalena: Released from Shame* immediately caught my attention.

This paper seeks to analyse and critique *Magdalena* to see how well or otherwise it presents the Gospel to an audience with a predominantly shame/honour mindset. I want to specifically consider the impact of this film on women from a shame/honour society, as such women are the film's target audience.

Communicating the Gospel in a Shame/Honour Society
Historically, western nations have interpreted the Gospel through the lens of a guilt/righteousness worldview, emphasising the cross's power to absolve us of our guilt.[3] Western missionaries have taken this interpretation and this good news all over the world. However, in most Muslim nations, this has not translated as good news but rather as irrelevant news.[4] Their felt problem is not guilt but shame. Muslim women, in particular, are also beset by fear.[5]

---

[1] Rebecca Hayman is a Melbourne based writer. Her latest novel *Career Advice for the Lost Soul* is a contemporary reconciliation story woven together with reflections on Luke's Gospel.

[2] Roland Muller, *The Messenger, the Message, the Community: Three Critical Issues for the Cross-cultural Church Planter*, Smashwords ed; n.p.: Independent Scholars Press, 2006, p309.

[3] Muller, p297.

[4] Muller, p277, 346.

[5] Phil & Julie Parshall, *Lifting the Veil: The World of Muslim Women*, Colorado Springs: Biblica, 2002, p14.

This apparent failure to communicate good news has led to the re-thinking of the power and message of the Gospel. It is now acknowledged that the Gospel has the power not only to absolve people from guilt, but also to release them from shame and fear. This three-fold victory over sin is written throughout the Bible but the average westerner with a guilt/righteousness mindset has required a new set of lenses to see it.[6]

Synopsis

The *Magdalena* film is set in 40AD Palestine and it retells the story of Jesus through the eyes of Mary Magdalena, out of whom Jesus drove seven demons. Magdalena begins her narration from Creation, explaining God's design and purpose. She then moves to Abraham, and God's promise to him and the meaning of sacrifice. Various prophets are mentioned after which Jesus is introduced.

The film deliberately focuses on events that involved women, such as the birth of Jesus, the women disciples, the miracles Jesus did for women, his interactions with women and the presence of the women at the cross and tomb.

Furthermore, Magdalena is in a house with women and children as she tells the story. Her analyses of events and the questions the women and children ask enrich and guide the narrative.

The film is overt, purposeful and unapologetic in its focus on women. For example, in one opening scene, the women are placed closest to Jesus. The camera pans over the faces of three women. Behind them are several men who are only partly visible to the audience. This is a typical crowd scene. The women are very visible.

A Film Predominantly for Muslims

Several factors make it clear that the film targets Muslims: its emphasis on a shame/honour combined with fear/power

---

[6] Muller, p304-5, p349.

worldview as well as the barriers it tries to deconstruct and the bridges it tries to construct.

Targeting those with a Muslim Worldview

As mentioned, the Muslim worldview is predominantly one of shame/honour but also one of fear/power. This is particularly true for Muslim women: many of whom feel they have already brought shame on the family just because they are female. *Magdalena* is clearly targeting this worldview.

The very words 'shame' and 'honour' are used in tandem a number of times. For example, '[Jesus] saw her shame and restored her honour' is a repeated phrase. 'Fear' is also mentioned a number of times. Magdalena says in summary, 'None of us need to live in fear or shame.' In contrast, 'guilt' is only mentioned once right at the end.

Many scenes highlighted by the film have that excruciating edge of shame. One particular scene, Joseph's discovery of Mary's pregnancy, is characterised by silence as he stares at her in horror. An audience from a shame-based culture would fill that silent pause with much meaning because Mary should be punished for that crime (Q24:2) and, in many countries, she would be killed.[7]

Similar to shame is the Muslim concept of purity. 'In almost all Islamic countries, it is strictly forbidden for men and women to touch in public.'[8] However, the film is insistent on depicting Jesus touching women because his touch demonstrates a further aspect of the Gospel's power, that being the power to make the unclean pure. From a Muslim perspective, a woman's body is 'shamefully polluting'. By touching a woman, especially the bleeding woman in Luke 8:43, Jesus shows that he doesn't see a woman's body as polluting.[9] In Muslim thought, defilement is contagious; if you touch something defiled you become defiled. The Gospel message is that Jesus involved himself with every form of defilement and

---

[7] Parshall & Parshall, p146.

[8] Parshall & Parshall, p.4-15.

[9] Miriam Adeney, *Daughters of Islam: Building Bridges with Muslim Women*, Illinois: Intervarsity Press, 2002, p122.

made them pure. Therefore, in Jesus, purity is contagious: to be touch by him, or by touching him, the person becomes pure.[10] Luke's account of the healing of the bleeding woman does not say that Jesus touched her; only that she touched him. *Magdalena*'s portrayal of Jesus' touch seems to emphasise this point about purity and defilement.

In terms of a fear/power paradigm, the film highlights Jesus' power through the miracles he performed. Driving of the demons out from Magdalena is particularly pertinent. This scene is deliberately slowed down, giving the audience time to witness Jesus' power over evil spirits. Millions of Muslim women, who are not well-grounded in orthodoxy, dabble in the occult and demonic possession is a well-known phenomenon.[11]

The film depicts another aspect of fear/power by using the symbol of a snake. At the beginning, the camera focuses on the snake tempting Eve, then again as Jesus is being whipped. Then, finally, it is shown dead by the wayside as Magdalena runs to tell the disciples that she has seen the risen Jesus. This symbolism graphically portrays Jesus' power.[12]

Deconstructing Barriers

The major barrier Muslims have to the Gospel is Christianity's insistence on the divinity of Jesus Christ (Q5:17). The film tackles this subject by introducing Jesus as Messiah, a common Qur'anic reference for Jesus[13] (4:171). It then dwells on Jesus' miraculous birth, which is also recorded in the Qur'an (3:47). At fourteen minutes into the movie, (hopefully everyone is riveted), Jesus is described as the 'Son of the Most High'. The narrative is interrupted for a discussion between Magdalena and one of her sceptical listeners Rivka.

---

[10] Moyra Dale, "Purity/Defilement." Paper presented at *When Women Speak*, Melbourne, 2015.

[11] Adeney, p75.

[12] *My Islamic Dream: Dream interpretation search engine.* http://www.myislamicdream.com.cited 9/10/15.

[13] Adeney, p66.

Rivka asks the question Muslims often ask of Christians, 'Surely you don't mean God had relations with a woman?'[14]

Magdalena of course denies this, re-explains the Holy Spirit's role and then says slowly, pointedly and unmistakeably: 'God is able to do anything? Don't you believe this?' This taps into Muslim belief that God can and will do whatever he wills. He is sovereign. It is a common Christian response to a Muslim's suggestion that God can't take human form.[15] Christian scholar John Azumah writes: 'God in Islam is all-powerful and almighty, capable of doing or wishing anything, yet he cannot have a son without having a wife? This is surely a serious limitation and an arbitrary restriction on the almighty and all-powerful God.'[16]

From this point on, the film unapologetically refers to Jesus as the Son of God as necessary, culminating with the high council accusing Jesus of claiming to be the Son of God. To which Jesus replies, 'You say that I am' (Luke 22:70).

The film makes an interesting extra-biblical point in relation to this issue of Jesus' divinity. In the synagogue scene of Luke 4, instead of a voice asking, 'Isn't this Joseph's son?' (Q4:22), the camera pans to a woman who asks: 'Isn't this Mary's son?' This is an unusual comment because, in Muslim society, a boy would be referred to as being the son of the father. However, 'son of Mary' is the Qur'an's most common designation for Jesus.[17]

Muslims believe that Jesus could not have been crucified because the Old Testament states: 'Cursed is anyone who hangs on a tree' (Deut 21:23). Jesus was a prophet, and therefore, God would not have cursed him. Islamic traditional understanding of the cross

---

[14] Phil Parshall, *New Paths in Muslim Evangelism: Evangelical Approaches to Contextualization*, Grand Rapids: Baker book House, 1980, p142.

[15] Adeney, p68.

[16] John Azumah, *My Neighbour's Faith: Islam explained for African Christians*, Kindle ed; Nairobi: Hippo Books, 2008), p2608/3340.

[17] Azumah, p2233/3340.

proposes various theories such as: God substituted Jesus for Judas; or Jesus was rescued from the cross and did not die.[18]

The film deals with this barrier in two stages. A Pharisee standing at the foot of the cross introduces the dilemma by quoting the curse. Later Magdalena analyses the text: 'The prophet Moses declared anyone hanging on a tree is cursed by God. When Jesus died upon the cross he took upon himself our curse: my curse of sin and death. His sacrifice and resurrection freed us from the clutch of evil, rescued us from the power of darkness and redeemed us from a life of fear and shame.' In this way, the film moves Jesus' death on the cross from being a controversy to being the crux of the message; Jesus was cursed and that is the point of the Gospel.

Finally, the film tries to tackle the Islamic understanding of God's transcendence and the unfortunate spin-off that God is neither interested nor involved in people's daily lives.[19] God's aloofness is particularly felt by women. 'Allah is simply not close, not real, not vital, nor practical to a woman's life. He is an abstract force to be obeyed, not loved. Intimacy with Allah is not part of a Muslim woman's thinking'.[20]

The film begins and ends with a statement of God's love and interest in the lives of all people, specifically women. At the start, the older friend of Magdalena wonders, as a woman, whether the Creator God would even see her let alone know her. 'Perhaps God Almighty would love a holy man,' she says. In conclusion, Rivka raises issue with Magdalena's assertion that God blesses all people. 'All people? Even women?' To which Magdalena responds: 'Jesus called me a daughter of Abraham. You are a cherished daughter; a daughter he wishes to bless ... None of us need to live in fear or shame. We no longer need to feel unseen or unheard.'

Building Bridges
The modest dress, mannerisms and culture of Palestine in 40AD, including veiled women and bearded men, are depicted

---

[18] Adeney, p71.

[19] Richard Shumack, *The Wisdom of Islam and the Foolishness of Christianity*, Sydney: Island View Publishing, 2014, p119-120.

[20] Parshall & Parshall, p225-6.

(fairly naturally) as being similar to traditional Muslim culture. A Muslim audience can therefore watch the film without feeling like their culture is under suspicion and scrutiny. On the contrary, their way of life is normalised and validated.[21] Similarly, the setting of women and children in a house, doing household tasks, is immediately relevant and endorsed.

One striking scene in the film comes across as a tribute to the Islamic veil. When Jesus refuses to condemn the woman caught in adultery (John 8), he lifts her fallen veil from the ground and covers her hair with it, signifying to a Muslim audience that Jesus is restoring her status as a modest and honourable woman.[22]

The film depicts Jesus and the religious leaders respecting the authority of Scripture and treating the actual scroll with honour; Jesus even kisses it before unwrapping it. This builds a bridge to a Muslim audience because they would treat the Qur'an with the exact same honour and respect.[23]

In line with Islamic sentiment, the film treats the prophets, in particular Abraham, with high esteem. In the scene of the sacrifice, Abraham's son is not named, thus a barrier is avoided because Muslim's believe Abraham offered Ishmael not Isaac.[24]

Finally, after Rivka has prayed to accept Jesus, the women instruct her to obey his Word, pray in faith, meet with those who follow and tell others about Jesus. These four things are delivered with such directness and authority that they seem to be presented as alternate but parallel practices to the 'Five Pillars'. Given Islam's emphasis on orthopraxis, I expect that a convert would be looking for what things she must 'do' in order to be a good Christian and the four things listed by the film are not unfamiliar practices to Islam.[25]

---

[21] Parshall, p115.

[22] E. Yuksel, L. S. al-Shaiban & M. Schulte-Nafeh (eds) *Qur'an: A Reformist Translation*, USA: Brainbow Press, 2007, p277.

[23] Parshall, p130.

[24] Parshall, p145.

[25] Azumah, p631/3340.

Is the Magdalena film Biblical?
The *Magdalena* film closely follows the life of Jesus as recorded in the Gospels. However, there are some slight changes and additions. 'Isn't this Mary's son?' has already been mentioned and seems to help further the point that Jesus' birth was unusual. Jesus touches women more than the biblical text explicitly states. Again this seems to be designed to further impress on viewers the point that Jesus does not regard women's bodies to be polluting. However, to my surprise, I found the extent to which he was portrayed touching women shocking. Possibly the producers have extended the point too far and have not sufficiently complied with the cultural norms of 40AD Palestine.

I object to the film following the NIV in its portrayal of John 8:11 'leave your life of sin', allowing the suggestion that the woman 'caught in adultery' was an immoral woman. Other translations go with the more problematic but seemingly more accurate translation: 'Go and sin no more.' I believe the NIV's rendition undermines the theological point John is making concerning Jesus' divinity. It also undermines the power of the scene in the film. The Gospel message in such a picture of Jesus covering the woman is that God raises us from shame to honour by covering us with a robe of righteousness.[26] This robe covers all shame not just the shame of prostitution as is implied by 'go and leave your life of sin'.

The importance of the phrase 'Son of God' has already been discussed. The film makes one slight change and adds one extra-biblical reference, seemingly to reinforce that Jesus' divinity is crucial to the Gospel. When Jesus is before the Sanhedrin, the film quotes Luke 22:70 with the chief priests asking: 'Are you then the Son of God?' However, instead of continuing the quote: 'You are right in saying I am', the film says: 'You say that I am.' To me this draws greater attention to people's response to the phrase 'Son of God'. The extra-biblical reference is even more striking. In the film, a chief priest says to Pilate: 'We have a law and by our law he ought to die because he claimed to be the Son of God.' I imagine a Muslim audience would agree; they also have such a law. To associate

---

[26] Muller, p422.

anyone with Allah as his partner (*shirk*) is the most heinous of sins (Q4:48; 31:13).[27]

There is a broader question revolving around the biblical legitimacy of using an evangelistic tool that targets women, when the Gospel is for all people. I contend that this is legitimate. Firstly, the film does not exclude men; it purposefully tries to include those who have traditionally been excluded. Secondly, Jesus stated that the focus of his ministry would be the poor and oppressed (Luke 4:18), who overwhelmingly happen to be women. (Around 70% of the world's poor are women).[28] In an interesting juxtaposition occurs in Luke 14. Jesus first instructs people to invite the poor [seven times out of ten, a woman], the crippled, the lame and the blind (v13) and then states that Heaven will be populated by the poor [women], the crippled the lame and the blind, not because others have not been invited, but because they have not responded (vv16-24). The testimony of Paul shows that this reality was already playing out in the New Testament church (1Cor 1:26-28). Thirdly, Jesus demonstrates a focus on women in his ministry. For example, notice the contrast between John 3 and 4. In John 3, a male leader approaches Jesus. Jesus speaks to him harshly and in riddles. In John 4, Jesus approaches a woman and gives her the clearest statement of his role and mission that anyone had yet received.

In a further comment on biblical evidence, Jesus also commissions women as evangelists, most famously Mary Magdalene (John 20:17). The evidence of John 4 shows that a woman, even a lowly one, can be an effective evangelist.

For all these reasons, I believe it is biblical to develop an evangelistic tool that focuses on women.

One final question to consider: Is it biblical to focus on shame and fear almost to the neglect of guilt? As already mentioned, *Magdalena* only mentions guilt once but uses 'shame' and 'fear' in tandem many times. Oddly, from the perspective of a western worldview, this ratio actually reflects the biblical narrative,

---

[27] 'Shirk (Islam)' *Wikipedia* https://en.wikipedia.org/wiki/Shirk_(Islam) cited 24/9/2015

[28] Matthew Maury. "Transforming Communities," *TEAR News: Women and poverty*, 1, 2014.

which does talk about shame and honour much more often than guilt. Honour is mentioned 190 times compared with guilt, which is only mentioned 40 times.[29] Furthermore, the foundational narrative 'the Fall' explicitly mentions shame and fear but guilt is only implied not stated (Genesis 3:7, 10). However, absolution from guilt is also a part of the Gospel's power and may need explanation rather than a passing reference.[30] It is also crucial to remember that, though the felt results may be guilt, fear and shame, the actual problem is sin.[31]

Is focusing on women an effective strategy for promoting the Gospel?

In some ways, this question is irrelevant if the approach has already been deemed biblical but it is still a debated point. The producers clearly feel that reaching women is worthwhile. In their words: 'Women worldwide can have great influence due to their spiritual openness, their social networks and their mothering roles. Reaching women and children is a tremendous strategy both globally and locally.'[32] Mothers are the main educators of their children as can be seen from this well-known Arabic saying: 'The mother is a school'.[33] Therefore, reaching women is also the best way to reach the next generation.

However, in contradiction to this strategy, Parshall writes: 'Muslim evangelism will not be successful as long as women, children and students comprise the convert community. Muslim men must be the target of evangelistic activity.'[34] He also says that, if the men aren't the initial converts, then Christianity will garner a poor image in the wider community.[35]

Parshall may be correct that the church would garner a poor image, however, as already stated above, Parshall is out of line with

---

[29] Muller, p411.

[30] Muller, p434.

[31] Muller, p523-525.

[32] *Women for Jesus: A Ministry of the Jesus film project*, 2015, http://www.womenforjesus.org cited 25/09/2015.

[33] Azumah, p1673/3340

[34] Parshall, p230.

[35] Parshall, p92.

biblical missionary strategy and Paul makes no suggestion that the church's 'poor image' is of any concern. Rather he expressly states that such a demographic is the fulfilment of the purposes of God (1 Cor 1:27-28). Ironically, Parshall is even out of step with his own lived experience that Muslim male converts don't bring their wives to church because they think they are too ignorant to understand.[36] Furthermore, though some male converts may tell their sons about the Gospel, they are unlikely to tell their daughters because these fathers will be giving their daughters in marriage to Muslim men.[37] Therefore, trying to spread the Gospel through the men will reach neither the older nor the younger women and possibly not even the next generation of men.

Adeney relegates Parshall's view to the category of popular myth.[38] She claims that it is a fallacy to assume the husband, the 'head' of the household, will draw the rest of the family to Christ. Women often see themselves as the conservators of religion who will keep their men on track as the men navigate the freedoms and temptations of the wider world. Furthermore, the women see it as their role to safeguard the children and keep them on the straight path of Islam. Adeney in fact argues for a relevant presentation of the gospel addressed specifically to women.[39]

I do want to note however Parshall & Parshall's sobering point that women are likely in serious danger if they convert without their male guardian's consent.[40] Apostasy is an offence for both women and men and both are in danger of being punished or killed (Q 4:89). But, on the whole, women are more vulnerable to acts of violence and every Christian worker needs to be mindful of the danger she may be posing for a Muslim woman. I think several factors need to be considered.

Firstly, the status of women, and hence their vulnerability, does vary across the Muslim world. For example, South East Asian

---

[36] Parshall & Parshall, p227-8.

[37] J. R. Meydan, *"Life Cycles: Stages in Women's Lives"*, Paper presented at When Women Speak, Melbourne, 2015.

[38] Adeney, p20.

[39] Adeney, p34-5.

[40] Parshall & Parshall, p247.

Muslim women are relatively important in their society,[41] particularly in the Philippines, which is quite matriarchal.[42]

Secondly, the status of women can vary according to their stage in life. For example, a Muslim woman in Bangladesh who has sons and daughters-in-law occupies a relatively powerful position in that society.[43] She may therefore be in less danger than a less powerful woman and yet be a more effective conduit of the Gospel than a man.

Finally, Christian workers need to be mindful of paternalism. Ultimately it is a Muslim woman's decision as to how much risk she is willing to expose herself to in pursuit of the Gospel. Conversion may be a long process and there should be no external pressure on a woman. It is up to the Holy Spirit to instruct her as to if and when she goes public about her conversion.[44]

Is the use of Film Effective?
There are two parts to this question. Firstly, *Magdalena* seems to be proving effective in terms of reaching women for Jesus. The *Magdalena* film's website lists many testimonials to its effectiveness.[45] One Christian worker (from a non-biased source) has used the film extensively among Muslim women in South East Asia. She found that the women related personally and deeply to the film. They would often comment: 'Even though these events happened a long time ago, it's talking about us.' For example, the Samaritan woman (John 4) spoke to some of them of their own felt shame of being second wives. Another woman was deeply moved by the story of the woman healed of bleeding. As a worker in Saudi Arabia, she had been badly treated and had had to flee for her life because she had suffered from a similar issue. Commonly the film would produce hours of discussion, as the women shared openly and often with tears about their experiences of shame. In facilitating discussion, the worker would ask the women: 'How do you see

---

[41] Adeney, p142.

[42] Beatrix Watofa, *Skype Interview* (26/8/2015).

[43] Meydan, "Life Cycles".

[44] Muller, p228, 235.

[45] *Women for Jesus: A Ministry of the Jesus film project*, 2015, http://www.womenforjesus.org/blog/category/story/magdalena/

Jesus dealing with this issue?' Often she would show the relevant part again and ask again: 'How does Jesus deal with this issue?' The women then were reaching their own conclusions about Jesus and seeing his remedy for shame.[46]

Generally, film does seem to be an effective means of evangelism. The *Jesus* film has reportedly touched the lives of millions of people in its thirty-year history. In some ways, the film is particularly helpful for women, because a disproportionate number of the world's illiterate people are women. Such women cannot avail themselves of Bibles and other literature, but can relate to film.[47] Adeney says that Muslim women learn the gospel better through creative means such as film. 'Balanced teaching, meaty teaching, can be understood and retained when imaginative media are used well.'[48]

The second aspect to consider is whether *Magdalena* is raising women to maturity in Christ and integrating them into Christian community. No film or any other mass media will likely do this in and of itself.[49] Therefore, follow-up is required, and the film should only be used as one tool to help people on their journey with Christ. In light of this problem, the producers have created a 12-episode Bible study video series called *Rivka,* especially for women who come to Christ as a result of watching *Magdalena*. The series is designed to be watched in small groups, with space for discussion. Quoting from the website: 'The spiritual response to *Magdalena* has been so great that supportive discipleship training has become a critical need, especially for women living in the least-reached regions of the world.'[50]

Availability
As part of the *Jesus* film media project, *Magdalena* taps into its networks and supports. *Magdalena* is included in the *Jesus* film

---

[46] Watofa. op. cit.

[47] *Women for Jesus,* http://www.womenforjesus.org/can-give/projects/#magdalena

[48] Adeney, p150.

[49] Muller, p762.

[50] *Women for Jesus.*

media app, which can be downloaded onto smart phones and then easily transported around the world. It is currently available in more than 100 languages.

Conclusion

Magdalena appears to be an extremely helpful tool for reaching Muslim women from a predominantly shame/honour worldview. It is an engaging media form, sympathetic to traditional lifestyles and respectful of many Islamic beliefs. It deliberately and explicitly aims to show the Gospel's power over shame and fear in an obvious attempt to minister to those struggling under this twin burden. That this burden is felt by many Muslim women is repeatedly demonstrated and attested to by the literature. However, it must be remembered, that Muslim women come from all walks of life and each worldview carries its individual stamp so users of *Magdalena* need to beware of the paternalistic trap of assuming every Muslim woman needs release from shame and fear. Furthermore, as a form of mass media, *Magdalena* is chiefly an evangelistic tool and further follow-up by Christian workers would be required to raise disciples.

By focusing on women with shame/honour worldviews, *Magdalena* is unlikely to speak as powerfully to men nor to speak as powerfully to women with other worldviews. But *Magdalena*'s focus is its strength. In a timely, intimately relevant and powerful way, it presents the Gospel to a sector of society often overlooked by missionary strategists.

Connecting with Muslims
Introducing *Mahabba*

Martin Schroeder[1]

Background

Founded in 2005 in Oxford UK, The *Mahabba* Network (called *Mahabba*) is a charity initiative that helps everyday Christians and Churches engage positively with Muslims through facilitating prayer and action.

Purpose

Mahabba's goal is to see Christians from all walks of life and across the denominations coming together in local groups for prayer, encouragement, and equipping, so they can build relationships with Muslim people in their communities.

The *Mahabba* Network

To date, *Mahabba* has established a network of 40 local prayer groups around the UK, which meet regularly and are involved with a variety of local projects and ministries. More recently, the network links have spread internationally to Southern Africa, France, Belgium, Norway, Austria and rapidly working into other European Nations. There are also growing links in Korea, India and Australia with a view to launching *Mahabba* groups in each country.

Leadership

Without burdening Church leaders with added responsibility, we aim through local coordinators to support those individuals who are being stirred to become involved. We start by encouraging them to pray together and link them to the skills, knowledge and insight of those who are experienced.

---

[1] Martin Schroeder is currently the representative for *Mahabba* here in Australia.

Vision
　　The task of equipping many more congregation members to reach out is enormous, but Mahabba aims to be a catalyst in partnership with others to create such an increased network of outreach.

Resources
　　For resources that are flexible and easily used in a wide variety of contexts, the *Mahabba* Network partners been developing equipping courses to support training and development in an easily accessible format. Previously one of the founders (Tim Green) compiled a course called "Friendship First" for ordinary Church members to gain understanding and we have just launched an equipping resource called "Joining the Family", which is designed to change the mind-set of Church leaders concerning the assimilation of Muslims into western churches.

Why is *Mahabba* needed?
Besides the huge international numbers of Muslim people in their home countries, over the last 30 years Muslim people have been migrating around the world and the migrated communities are growing significantly.

International examples
　　There are around 1,500 mosques in the UK and 2.7 Muslims, which by 2020 is projected to grow 5.5 million across the nation.

　　In the United States, the Muslim population is projected to more than double in the next 20 years, from nearly 2.6 million in 2010 to about 6.2 million in 2030, and accounting for 1.7% of the population. This is estimated to be a larger number than any other European country (other than Russia and France).

　　In Europe itself, the Muslim population is projected to exceed 58 million by 2030, making up 8% of the population. Most will continue to live in eastern Europe, but some of the biggest increases are expected to occur in France, Italy and Germany.

Why *Mahabba* in Australia?
In Australia, the growth of the Muslim population is also expected

to be significant with approximately 550,000 people representing between 2.2 - 2.4% of the national population. Islam is the second fastest growing faith group in the country after Hinduism.

The more recent arrival of Muslims from conflict impacted nations provides a great opportunity to reach out to people who are earnestly seeking a deeper life in God, desperate to find a sense of belonging in a land alien to their own and find a new sense of purpose for their lives.

In summary

Mahabba seeks to build a positive and viable alternative to current responses of fear, ignorance, apathy, or even violence and by building a persistent prayer network and support network to equip thousands of ordinary Christians and local church networks.

Contacting *Mahabba*
In terms of contacting *Mahabba* the best process is as follows

1. Find a Group - to join for prayer, enquirers should contact me and I will try to link them to a group or help set one up locally.

2. Set up a group - please contact me and I will assist them with a coordinators toolkit and support them to set it up.

3. Obtain Training Resources - they can click on the resources tab and select be directed to portals that will provide links to very resources.

4. Find other support or information - they can contact me directly by phoning or emailing at the contact details below.

Martin Schroeder
Mahabba Australia
mahabbanetwork.com
t: +61 (0) 406 717711

Reflections

Mission 2 Australian Muslims (M2AM) Conference

In mid-March, 2016 the *Australian Christians Responses to Islam* group held their annual conference M2AM in Sydney. Delegates came from every state in Australia except the Northern Territory. It was also an international gathering with many countries and nations represented, including a number who had found Christ and who were from various Muslim backgrounds.

The weekend program was well balanced between formal sessions and opportunities for interaction and conversation with others sharing similar interests. The main sessions were led by Tim and Rachel Green, both of whom have been actively engaged in discipleship ministries to those seeking Christ from Muslim backgrounds. The sessions were practical and covered such issues as Identity, Belonging and Discipleship. Another session looked at the distinctiveness involved in discipling men and women from Muslim cultural backgrounds. Another very practical session involved a brief survey of a whole range of different methods for evangelism. There were also a number of elective sessions. The session on "one on one mentoring across cultures" was again very practical and insightful. Dr Catherine Power's presentation on "Grief and Trauma" was focused on personal care for those who are involved in ministry, which often involves interaction with grief and trauma.

The conference also included times of worship and the meeting room filled with the sounds of praise. A number of the songs were in other languages and their words (translations were given) gave powerful testimonies. What a joy it was too to be led in devotion by one of the brothers whom God had called out of Islam!

Tim and Rachel also introduced three very valuable resources. Two of the resources are relevant to Christians wishing to reach out in love to their Muslim neighbours; "Friendship First" and "Joining the Family." Another resource which Tim Green has developed is "Come Follow Me", a discipleship tool which can be used with Muslim converts who have a reasonably good grasp of English. Both resources are available through INTERSERVE, Australia.

SEVERAL OTHER RESOURCES[1]

Bridges is a course which is available through Middle East Christian Outreach and suggests ways for reaching out to Muslim friends and neighbours.

Magdalena is a film which uses Mary Magdalene to introduce Muslim women to Jesus Christ in a very sensitive manner. It is available from the makers of the Jesus film.

---

[1] These resources are mentioned for the information of readers only and are not necessarily endorsed or recommended by the CSIOF.

When Women Speak Colloquium[1]

At the end of September 2015, in a partnership between Interserve Australia, Interserve International, CMS and Melbourne School of Theology, the *When Women Speak Colloquium* was held on the outskirts of Melbourne for the purpose of 'exploring the place of women's voices where Christianity, Islam and missiology meet'.

The colloquium brought together thirty women from sixteen nationalities with experience in more than fourteen nations where Islam is the dominant religion. It embraced women across ages, experienced and less experienced, as well as welcoming followers of Jesus from a Muslim background, second generation believers, and those from a Christian background. This was a rich mix of women with a passion to see Jesus made known among one of the most marginalised groups in our world today, Muslim women.

Six keynote papers were presented, with two main respondents to each paper. Many of the women were scholar-practitioners who have engaged with the academic in order to develop their understanding of ministry in their Muslim context. They commented on the joy of being invited into a space where their contribution was welcomed, and they were affirmed in their gifting, scholarship and ministry.

Worship was very intentionally placed at the centre of the colloquium, and while this was at times, for some, unusual and not always comfortable, God was pleased to come among us. In meeting with God, women found healing and renewal, refreshment and fresh vision.

Creative gifts of the women were also released enhancing the environment in which the meetings were held, reflecting a side that is often absent from academic gatherings. Many wonderful

---

[1] Reprinted here with thanks to "When Women Speak".

volunteers supported the colloquium in a myriad of ways with their gracious hospitality - a true reflection of community in action.

The venue for dinner on Friday night at the Melbourne School of Theology had been appropriately and beautifully decorated by gifted creative women. There, more than 150 guests embraced the opportunity to hear from participants, to grow their understanding of ministry among Muslim women, and to pray with and for those who focus in this area. It was also the platform to launch the Vivienne Stacey Scholarship which is committed to equipping Christian women from the Middle East, Asia and Africa to do higher research in Islam.

Saturday afternoon was spent exploring the way forward, following through from what was learned each day together. It was both humbling and awe-inspiring to see how God met with us, confirming at least 80% of the things some of us had been sensing beforehand as the way ahead. So, we continue to pray and work towards the development and growth of a network of women scholar practitioners engaged collaboratively in research and resource development on issues of Jesus and Muslim women; of local focus groups being formed both geographically and in research and ministry interest areas; of mentoring a new generation of women who live out God's grace and love for women who live under Islam; of bringing Muslim women back to an open space where they might find and experience God's gracious love; and of supporting and mentoring Christian women in their journey to be equipped to engage with the Muslim world.

There is a book to produce, a webzine to develop, together with a blog to engage discussion, and training resources to equip the many who have a growing heart for reaching Muslim women. God is good, and we look to him as we explore registering *When Women Speak*, partnering with organisations and individuals who want to share the journey. A first step in sharing more widely the expertise gathered at the colloquium was the training day held on Monday, where fifteen of the colloquium participants offered their insights and experience to over 70 people who came from all across Australia.

The program was graciously supported by organisations and individuals in a variety of ways, which included financial gifts, prayer, hosting participants, and promoting the events associated with *When Women Speak*. The result: women were encouraged to use their gifts and calling to engage with Muslim women. At times the challenges faced in endeavouring to organise the event were almost overwhelming, but praise God, the event took place.

Yet, there is still much to be done. If you are interested in knowing more about this initiative contact:

From "When Women Speak"
admin@whenwomenspeak.net, or
www.whenwomenspeak.net.

Muslim Christian Panel Report

Description of Event

On the 27th of March 2015 a debate was held at the Ringwood East Uniting Church between two Muslims and two Christians/human rights activists. The Muslims were represented by Ali Derany (a Shia Muslim), and Sheikah Wadud Janud (Ahmadiyya Muslim). Vickie Janson the Victorian Director of the Australian Christians Political Party and Elizabeth Kendal a Human Rights Activist were present on the panel. The atmosphere was polite and settled with an audience of more than 250 attentively listening to all speakers. At the beginning, the moderator of the panel Bernie Powers indicated that the purpose of the event this was a peaceful discussion with both sides of the panel sharing their views.

Each panel member introduced themselves and talked for about three minutes on what their key message for the audience members would be. Bernie (the moderator) then facilitated questions and responses on the comparisons of Islam. Some of these topics included views on Jesus, Muhammad, the Bible and the Qur'an. Jesus was discussed as being a prophet but not the Son of God, Ali Derany spoke of the word and teachings of Jesus as being relevant. This then led into a discussion as to whether Jesus was crucified and killed, or not? The Muslim panellists had slightly differing beliefs: one stated that he was neither crucified nor killed and the other stating that although he was crucified he did not die.

Muhammad was viewed as a prophet who was chosen as a prophet because he was perfect. Had he not been perfect he would have been a hypocrite. Vickie Janson questioned this logic, while Janud stated that being perfect does not mean that you don't have shortcomings.

Each person was relatively articulate with their points. However, due to a lack of time a number of topics were not covered. Once the comparisons had been made between Islam and

Christianity, the panel answered questions from the audience sent in via text message. The topics that were covered in the question time included: the beheading of 600 people by Muhammad, the correct translation of the Qur'an and women in relation to Islam. In relation to this last topic the discussion included the banning of the burqa, discrimination and the difference between faith and culture. Concerning the burqa, some considered it a cultural rather than religious requirement. Vickie pointed out that Australians can find it offensive since 'so much covering' is not part of our culture.

The main direction of the discussion was an explanation and defence of Islamic beliefs. The Christian viewpoint was mentioned but only in response to what Janud and Ali had said. The Qur'an was used and referred to as the Holy Book. There were disagreements as to which was the 'correct' translation. It was stated that only the original text of the Qur'an was the 'correct' version and that the English translations were not reliable nor true.

At the end of the question time each person was asked to summarise and tell the audience what their desires for the future were. Vickie focused on the freedom of speech and the freedom of belief, and the importance of making sure that laws are not introduced that prevent these. Ali's main message was that we need to make the world a better place through love and caring. He pointed out that one of the ways to do this was to know ourselves so that we can know others. Elizabeth was passionate about the persecuted church and the need for peace and the possibility of achieving this through prayer. Janud made a point that he felt that the panel went about the discussions the wrong way. What is needed is that we all need to have the intention of understanding their (Muslim) beliefs while not trying to pick at them. He suggested befriending a Muslim so that we can understand their belief and culture as well as break-down some of the barriers that might exist.

At the end, Bernie concluded by thanking everyone for coming and participating in a peaceful debate/discussion about Islam and Christianity.

Response
The concept of having a panel discussion on the differences/similarities between Islam and Christianity is a positive move; it allows both sides in the discussion to state their points of

view in a way that is not confrontational or argumentative. I do not believe that it is necessarily better than a formal debate; I think that both have their place. However, it seems easier to facilitate a peaceful discussion than a peaceful debate. Having a panel allows for more than two points of view to be represented and gives the audience a greater chance to ask questions.

The panel was relatively balanced with two Christian points of view and two Muslim points of view. It would have been helpful to have a panellist who was a former Muslim. They could share their view from a perspective of having lived in both worlds. As I understand it two former Muslims were invited but unfortunately, due to unforeseen circumstances, were unable to make it.

Each panellist was eager to answer questions and state their opinion while also allowing the other panellists to share theirs. At one point in the evening tensions did rise because of the views expressed but the situation did not escalate. Vickie was strong in her beliefs advocating for Christians and interjecting at some claims that Ali and Janud had made. One interjection related to Muhammad, querying how he could be a perfect man and have shortcomings. Ali was well spoken and somewhat gentler in his approach. He came across as someone who did not want to argue and appeared to be more open to other people's beliefs.

Janud as a scholar of Islam presented himself as someone who wanted to defend every belief/point discussed from his point of view. His answers were long and at times off track, dragging the conversation out and limiting the amount of questions that could have been answered. His view of the Qur'an was that it is only the Arabic version that was correct and that English translations were not acceptable. At one stage Vickie quoted from a Qur'an that had been produced in Saudi Arabia, but he refused to believe/acknowledge her point as, he claimed, she was quoting from the wrong Qur'an. It appears that Saudi Arabia has beliefs that he does not accept (i.e. beheadings and not allowing women to drive). He claims that these state beliefs have been imposed into their translations of the Qur'an, and therefore those translations cannot be considered a true one. I felt that he found it difficult to handle views that diverged from his. He came across as quite dogmatic at times.

Bernie, as a moderator, facilitated the discussion well, allowing a good number of topics to be covered. I think that some people were allowed to express their views more than others and so tended to dominate the conversation. As the moderator he could have taken a stronger stand to move the conversation on to other topics rather than allowing the panel to get caught up in the topic that was being discussed.

All the topics discussed were main issues that are commonly raised concerning the Islamic faith. Personally, I felt that both Muslims were quick to dismiss the questions simply on the basis of not knowing enough about the topic. One of the questions that was raised was in relation to the beheading of 600 people. Before eventually answering the question, Janud believed that he didn't have to. However, he did acknowledge that for people who had very little understanding of the issue, it was a valid question.

I found the discussion about women and Islam one of the more interesting topics. I felt that the answers given appeared to twist the truth. Even when challenged I felt that the points of disagreement were not considered. It seems to me that the Islamic faith makes statements that obviously contradict what is actually written in the Qur'an but when challenged about it, simply states that we are reading from the wrong translation.

As mentioned previously I felt that Janud was quite outspoken and did not allow other ideas to be expressed. I felt that Elizabeth should have had more of an opportunity to speak but it is almost impossible to allow each person to have an equal share of the 'floor'.

From this evening I gained a better understanding of what Muslims believe and how they interpret the Qur'an. Personally, I became aware of a number of contradictions. It also seemed that some ideas were expressions of their beliefs rather than the teaching of the Qur'an. I believe that the evening was worthwhile. I was surprised at how much I knew, and that I recognised some of the typical arguments/ responses that were used to defend the Islamic belief.

In terms of future events I would suggest a stricter observance of the time limits, and an enforcing of adherence to the topic in question. Often information shared did not seem entirely relevant to the topic being discussed. Over all, people gained helpful insights through allowing those attending to openly and honestly discuss their beliefs and culture. In this way they shed some light on, and dispelled, some of the misconceptions that people have about Islam.

M. Morris
MST Student

Christian Perspectives on a Buddhist Theme
A visit to the Wat Thai

Chee Seng Fah [1]

Our visit to Wat Thai Melbourne was an insight into Buddhism and significant for our study of that religion. It enabled us to take our learning and see it in the context of a living faith in real people's lives. Overall the visit was informative, confusing and also different to what I had expected.

A Summary of the Visit
The Buddhist temple is not a large 'temple-like' construction, but rather comprises three properties in the residential hub of Box Hill. These properties have been purchased over time and joined together. Each of the three houses has a different function and includes rooms for worship and meditation. The 'general' room (a living room) is used as a 'counselling' room for the monk and his members. This is where we spent most of our time in discussion.

Another larger separate building is used for functions, ceremonies and meditation. The third room is an open room attached to the third house. This open room is also used for meditation, functions and ceremonies. In each of these 'rooms' there is an altar with a statue of Buddha at the centre as well as a picture of the founder of the temple, His Holiness Phra Dhammakunaporn.

Somewhat surprising was a fourth altar which was set up in a room adjacent to the kitchen of the first house. It was different in that it had a myriad of other statues which included Brahman and Buddha with Kuan Yin. The latter was the largest and was

---

[1] Chee Seng Fah serves as an associate pastor at Clayton Church of Christ. His passion is to teach/preach the Word of God and to equip others to do the ministry.
He was a past student of MST.

positioned in the centre of the altar. The altar was being used as a place of worship which included incense, fruit and flowers as offerings for these and various other 'bodhisattvas'. This reflects elements of folk religion to which we will return to later.

The head monk of the temple welcomed us briefly and unexpectedly referred us to his assistant to answer our questions because of his poor English. His assistant is the chair of the Buddhist Council of Victoria and a member of the temple. We spent the next hour discussing the Buddhist faith with her, while the head monk meditated in the same room. At the end of our discussion, he farewelled us and summed up Buddhism by saying, 'Buddhism is a D.I.Y. religion'. After the discussion, we had some time exploring the other parts of the property.

A Theravada Buddhist Temple

This Buddhist community is based on the Theravada stream originating from a missionary movement out of Thailand. The founding monk had a vision of promoting the teachings of Buddha in the western world, and this temple was established with the support of the local community of Asian and Thai Buddhists. The assistant also spoke about the two distinctives that are unique to Thai Theravada Buddhism: the altar set up[2] and the availability of the head monk as a 'sitting monk'[3].

Despite their affiliation with the Theravada stream, the community provides for people whose beliefs embrace elements of Mahayana and folk Buddhism. Some have faith in bodhisattvas[4], in this case Kuan Yin, who is considered the bodhisattva of compassion (Avalokiteshvara)[5]. They also hold the belief that enlightenment is for all people. These beliefs are distinctive to Mahayana Buddhism which is in contrast to Theravada Buddhism

---

[2] Thai altars use a small Buddha in comparison with Sri Lankan Buddhist altars that use a large Buddha.

[3] The 'sitting monk' not only focuses on meditation, but is also more accessible to people to serve them in spiritual matters.

[4] Bodhisattva – "In Mahayana Buddhism, a person who has achieved enlightenment, but has chosen to remain in this world to help those who are suffering instead of going on to nirvana. This is the highest ideal. The idea of the bodhisattva is contrasted to the *arhat* of Theravada Buddhism".

[5] There is a folk belief that *Kuan Yin* keeps people safe from natural catastrophe. http://www.buddhanet.net/e-learning/history/kuanyin-txt.htm cited 27 January, 2015.

where the emphasis is on becoming an *arahat*[6] while maintaining that enlightenment is only accessible by a few (Halverson: 56).

The community also worshipped the four-faced Hindu god Brahma (common in Thailand) and known there as Phra Phrom. This reflects syncretistic aspects of folk Buddhism through beliefs in other deities. The assistant explained that while the Brahma deity existed before 'Buddha's time', it learned Buddha's essential teachings of compassion, joy, and lovingkindness from the 28 other Buddhas who preceded the last teaching Buddha.[7]

It was confusing to see these syncretistic elements within this Thai stream of 'Theravada' Buddhism. However, the assistant explained that since Buddhism is 99% psychology it accepts that people create things in their mind which makes them comfortable and helps them. Sometimes it is difficult for such people to see past the world's illusion and realise that what they have is a creation of their own mind. So it doesn't matter whether it is Brahma, Kuan Yin, or whether there is an apparent hierarchy on the altar since this is what the mind creates. What is important is that these people receive equal respect while helping them to realise that the true Buddhist teaching is about your mind and yourself. Such reasoning suggests that Thai Buddhism has the same capacity as Hinduism to absorb all religions into itself, including Christianity, on the basis of psychology.

Christian Response to Key Doctrines
In spite of the confusion regarding where the institution sits within the spectrum of Buddhism, the assistant outlined the doctrines that were consistent with the essentials of Buddhism. It is clear that Christianity has some areas of common ground with Buddhism but there are points of differences that make them incompatible. These will be discussed under the following key doctrines.

Four Noble Truths

---

[6] '*Arahat (arhat)* is one who is more concerned with his own enlightenment than with that of others. His primary concern is to attain enlightenment for himself by forsaking all illusion.'. D C Halverson, The Compact Guide to World Religions, Minnesota, Bethany House Publishers, 1996, p56.

[7] These buddhas understood and practised the philosophy but just couldn't articulate the teachings and philosophy like the last Buddha.

The assistant identified the core beliefs of Buddhism in the four noble truths: there is suffering, the origin of suffering, an end to suffering and a path out of suffering.[8] Christianity similarly recognizes the suffering in the world, how desire can cause suffering, the vain pursuit of the temporal and the need to be free from the suffering of this world. However, where Buddhism sees suffering as the result of desire and karma, Christianity attributes it to our fallen nature and sin. In fact, *desiring* to eliminate desire is difficult to attain. Jesus recognized that the issue is not the eliminating of desire altogether but rather having the right desire (Matthew 5:6). In Buddhism the goal is to detach oneself from the temporal while projecting the idea of Self into the permanence of Nirvana, but Christianity finds permanence in our eternal relationship with God. Being in Him means that we don't have to detach ourselves, but rather, we can engage and find hope in our hardships, contentment in our poverty and the freedom to forgive personal insults. Ultimately, the cross of Christ enables us to find life in the midst of suffering. While Buddhism looks to the eightfold path as the way of 'salvation', Christianity looks to a faith-based relationship.

Eightfold Noble Path and The Five Precepts

The assistant explained that the way to avoid dissatisfaction with life is through the eightfold noble path: right views and right thoughts (wisdom), right speech, right actions, right livelihood (ethics), right effort, right mindfulness and right concentration (meditation).[9] She also spoke about the five precepts: 1) to abstain from taking life 2) to refrain from stealing 3) to avoid sexual immorality 4) to refrain from lying and 5) to abstain from all intoxicants. [10]

Christianity similarly recognizes the need for wisdom, morality and the renewal of the mind (Romans 12:1-2). In fact, the five precepts represent the Buddhist equivalent of the Ten Commandments. However, Buddhism fulfils the eightfold path through a self-reliant morality. It is a self-salvation and work-based

---

[8] V.A Sumedho, The Four Noble Truths, (Buddha Dharma Education Association Inc.) http://www.buddhanet.net/pdf_file/4nobltru.pdf cited 4 June, 2015, p9.

[9] Britannica Encyclopaedia of World Religions, Chicago, 2006, p433-463

[10] J Dickson, A Spectator's Guide to World Religions, Sydney South, Blue Bottle Books, 2004, p71.

religion. However, unlike Buddhism, Christianity is dependent on the work of Christ alone, who died for our sins. Our salvation is dependent on faith in Jesus Christ and not human effort (Romans 3:23-26). Salvation is a gift from God to us and a person cannot work for their salvation (Ephesians 2:8-10).

Rebirth

When the doctrine of rebirth was discussed, it appeared to be a difficult teaching for the assistant to articulate. She explained that rebirth was different from Hindu reincarnation because there was no 'self'. It is the realization of the illusion of 'self' that enables us to be freed from suffering. When asked what comes back in the rebirth cycle, she answered 'seven treasures': characteristics that continue on as a flow of consciousness into the next physical body, such as generosity and compassion. Other Buddhist teachings mention the five aggregates of human existence. These include: matter (*rupa*), sensation (*vedana*), perception (*samjna*), mental formations (*samskara*) and consciousness (*vijnana*).[11] Christianity, however, emphasizes that we are made in the image of God (Genesis 1:26) and hence our personal existence is real (not an illusion) and has value and worth. The Bible teaches that we continue to exist as persons after our death.

The assistant also indicted that life continues after death because of the karmic saying, "we always come with two baskets of good deeds and bad deeds. You can never clear your bad basket. Whatever you have done will always carry into the next life." In contrast the cross of Jesus Christ enables our bad baskets to be cleared once and for all. The forgiveness of Jesus enables our past sins to be buried with Him and raises the believer to walk in 'newness of life' (Romans 6:4) in this life and eternity.

The God Idea

The assistant explained that Buddhism does not believe in a god and Buddha is not a god but a teacher. In fact, gods are a creation of people's minds in order to help themselves. She also mentioned that there are questions that Buddha doesn't answer, such as supernatural matters like creation and life after death. Rather the Buddha asks in return, 'what is your purpose for knowing?'

---

[11] Dickson, pp57-58 BEWR, p148

However, in spite of that statement, it was explained that Buddhists still believe that there is something more powerful than us and that is the Buddha. In addition, Chinese Buddhist traditions believe there is still a heaven and earth, and that spirit *devas* exist around people to guide and control them and they can be called upon for help. Such Buddhist views seek to provide answers to some fundamental questions surrounding creation, destiny and the human need for a higher being.

Summary

In conclusion, the assistant made this surprising statement that you can be a practising Christian and Buddhist at the same time on the grounds that Buddhism is a philosophy aiming to live morally. Nevertheless, while there may be points of commonality, at the core Buddhism is still incompatible with Christianity. While Christianity is often accused of making the exclusive claim that Jesus is 'the way, the truth and the life', Buddhism makes a similar claim. It embraces all different religions, but only on the premise that *karma* is everything and everything else is illusion.

Paying a visit to Hare Krishna

Janaya Wattie[1]

The Hare Krishna movement grew to prominence in the West in the 1970s, when many young Westerners were turning East in their spiritual search, under the influence of the current fashion and a desire to distance themselves from the ways of their parents. The Hare Krishna appeal has waned in recent decades, yet their presence is still here on our streets and in our suburbs if we care to look.

So it was with a sense of considerable curiosity that I went with a group to visit a temple in Albert Park, Melbourne, belonging to the Hare Krishna movement, more officially called the ISKCON (International Society for Krishna Consciousness Inc.). It was a day of challenges and questions.

I had many expectations before going to the temple. I expected to see many idols and shrines to numerous deities, in particular a major idol to Vishnu "the Keeper", who some believe to be an avatar[2] of Krishna. I didn't know the difference between the Hare Krishnas and Hinduism, so I expected to be informed of the difference and perhaps challenged by their arguments regarding their faith. I expected a fancy and elaborate building that looked clearly like a temple. Inside I thought I'd be surrounded by a myriad of colour, stone-work and paintings displaying the great epics – Ramayana and Mahabharata. I also expected a strong smell of incense and to hear Indian-style music. I expected to observe a relaxed atmosphere, little corporate structure; people meandering back and forth in individualistic worship, participating in various

---

[1] Janaya Wattie graduated from MST in 2015 (after 9 years of study!) and is married with 2 young children.

[2] Ed note: 'avatar' in Hindu mythology is the descent of a deity to the earth in an incarnate form or some manifest shape; the incarnation of a god.

rituals – bowing and chanting mantras, possibly participating in yoga. I thought the women would be wearing brightly coloured, Indian-style clothing and lots of gold (or apparent gold) jewellery. I expected references to the sacred texts, *karma* and *moksha* (freedom from the cycle of *samsara*, or rebirth).

Events on the visit

We arrived and presented ourselves at the reception. The building was an old Victorian style house converted into a temple. Thus from the outset, my experience was different from what I expected. From the outside, there was no obvious appearance that the building was a temple, although there was a large sign announcing it as ISKCON. The building still retained the air and charm of a large Victorian mansion. A strong smell of curry permeated the air.

After speaking briefly with the Temple President, we were led to the 4pm service (known as an *arti*) in the temple, which is separated from the administration building by a courtyard. Part of the courtyard contained a garden which encompassed a fountain and two elephants that appeared to 'guard' its entrance.

There are six *arti* services each day, with those in the early morning and early evening being the best attended. As the one we observed was still in work hours, there were very few people there.

In the foyer of the temple we were asked to remove our shoes. The main area of the temple was an open room, with a marbled floor and intricate sculptured work all around the inside architraves. The sculpted work was of vine-like floral designs and lion heads on one side above the screen. This was all painted in pale pink and green, giving the temple a 'soft' atmosphere. I found the colour and decoration of the temple quite beautiful. The marbled floor contained the design of a flower in the centre. There was only one main statue in the main temple. This was a lifelike statue of the founder of the Hare Krishna faith - Srila Prabhupada. There were approximately a dozen pictures on the walls of various people and deities. On the wall opposite the statue of the founder was a screen, behind which was the inner sanctum/temple. Within the inner temple were three statues of Krishna in a row. In the centre was Krishna and his wife; one the left was a Lord and his "second" (partner in his work while on the right was another form of Krishna. There was a smell of incense but it was not overpowering.

Each temple devotee first entered, bowed, and prostrated themselves on the floor towards the large statue of Srila Prabhupada. During the service, there were hymns (not just instrumental music) played on a stereo and the temple priestess continually rang a bell. Food was also offered to the idols before we arrived. At one point a conch shell was sounded for a few minutes. The priestess then handed out (through the screen) some rose-heads to a devotee who then passed them around to us.

Talking with the President
After observing the devotions, we returned to meet with the Temple President. His office contained a few statues and pictures hanging on the walls. It was spacious, and not overly cluttered despite the many objects and books within it. It also had comfortable couches to sit on which helped relieve some of my nervousness.

Our discussion ranged over many topics. The President quickly established that we were Christians (he said he could tell we were Christians by our "look"). However, once he realised that we were there to learn about his faith and not 'Bible Bash' or forcibly convert him, he relaxed and was sincere in trying to help us understand the perspectives he held on various issues.

We were informed that the two main differences that distinguish Hare Krishnas from mainstream Hinduism is their rejection of the caste system and their belief in monotheism. The founder of Hare Krishna (Srila Prabhupada) was against the caste system, teaching that it was a "perversion of Scripture". The President explained that a person is not born into a rank, but rather people are born with a particular 'make-up', born with particular qualities which make them best suited to various professions (i.e. a person may be born with a flair for business, (i.e. having strong business skills, enjoying the profession and doing well hence remaining in that position). Their view of monotheism is that Krishna is the original form and is supreme, with other deities underneath who are not to be worshipped directly. He also said that Vishnu (one of Hinduism's major gods) was a form of Krishna.

The president proceeded to give us an overview of the Hare Krishna's history, and explained how his order had developed out of Hinduism.

Another distinctiveness of the Hare Krishna movement is its dedication to mission and preaching. They strive to convert people through 'chanting parties' and through the distribution of books which explain their beliefs.

The temple we went to visit is one of the largest in Australia, with approximately 4000 families that are connected with it (most are described as 'sympathisers'), while approximately 100-120 of those families take an active role in the temple as priests, administration staff and so forth.

The President then went on to relate his personal testimony – how he had had a Christian upbringing, got involved in the 'hippie movement' and then heavily into drugs, including dealing. He related how no-one had been able to answer his questions on the purpose of life and who he really was. However, he found answers in the Hare Krishna people who accepted him as he was and encouraged him to get involved. During this he explained various points of belief such as all material things having a 'spiritual side' and how their goal is to free themselves from their bondage to the cycle of birth and death.

He also talked about Hare Krishna views on purification and sin. To them, purification is the process of identifying with one's spiritual consciousness rather the one's material consciousness. The analogy given was that of a pure water droplet (our original spiritual state) falling on dirt. This combination makes mud (our present state). The goal of a Hare Krishna is to re-identify with spiritual consciousness (i.e. get back to pure water) – to release the soul from bodily form. Beginning to understand their concept of sin required learning their beliefs in *karma* – actions which give positive, negative or neutral responses (good *karma*, bad *karma* or *akarma*[3] respectively). They believe that we desire to sin – the

---

[3] Ed note: "Akarma" means "inaction", according to GK Marballi, Journey Through The Bhagavad Gita - A Modern Commentary With Word-To-Word Sanskrit-English Translation, Azure Publishing, 2013, p102.

activities which produce negative *karma*. We can get rid of the activity, but not the desire to sin. This desire comes due to our ignorance of our spiritual condition and forgetfulness of our original position as a servant of God. Interestingly, devotional activities are seen as *akarma*, not positive *karma*. However, as the President went on to explain, a Hare Krishna follower actually wants neither positive nor negative *karma*, but rather *akarma* in order to break out of the circle of *samsara*.

Another topic we discussed was the clothing that they wear. The receptionist wore colourful Indian-style clothing, with lots of jewellery and piercings, while the President wore a white outfit. This also identifies them with the Hare Krishna faith. Similarly, each day they put clay markings on their faces to declare their beliefs.

We ended the discussion cordially after approximately one hour. In a further email, the President explained that the food offered in the temple was considered sacred and then later given to any devotees who were hungry. The flowers given in the service were also part of the offering and therefore considered sacred. He also mentioned that the mark on a lady's forehead is a symbol of her married state. In the discussion, he said that a requirement of an initiate or those who wish to be initiated was to be celibate. The president also explained that while preaching (and 'devotional activities) were akarma, they were still considered important in order to encourage people to *"free themselves from the bondage to the cycle of birth & death"*. He finally affirmed that they have a personal relationship with God and said that people have *"just forgotten it"*. (thus it is viewed in a different sense to how a Christian would understand it).

Thoughts for Christian Visitors to Hare Krishna Temples
The visit posed many different kinds of challenges. First was the concern I felt that someone like the President, with an apparent 'traditional high church' background, could have so clearly missed the central point of faith in God. Nor had he, when searching as a young man, been able to find any Christian who could adequately answer his questions on spirituality. It also stunned me that his testimony sounded like many I have heard in a Christian church service, and Christian visitors to Hare Krishna temples should anticipate this.

I was impressed with the president's attempts to genuinely answer our questions, although I was not remotely convinced by his arguments! He was patient, hospitable and very kind, a feature of the Hare Krishna movement which is central to their own mission strategies.

The Hare Krishna faith appears to be very much a works-based faith, working towards personal freedom, but of a different type to the Christian faith which accepts a freedom through God's grace. Their concept of sin is also different. As Christians, we would not attribute all sin to ignorance (we would argue that humans often knowingly do wrong). We would also hold different views on Jesus' divinity (this was discussed with the President). We would stress that he is the Son of God, rather than just an "empowered teacher" or "servant of God" or even a "prophet". Also, our views on the compatibility of an interfaith meeting would differ greatly. While we (along with Muslims and Jews) would struggle to overlook certain doctrinal differences (such as the divinity of Jesus), the President had no problem with accepting these.

Overall it was a worthwhile experience and I am pleased that I had the opportunity to attend.[4] There was too much to look at and absorb in one visit, but it was good exposure to a very different faith. Having said that, I felt uncomfortable several times and would not have liked to have gone on my own. The Hare Krishna followers we spoke with clearly saw our visit as an opportunity for their own mission. So Christians considering undertaking such a visit should prepare themselves beforehand with information on the movement and with answers to the challenges they are likely to face, and they should also make the visit in the company of fellow believers.

---

[4] For further information on the Hare Krishna, see Christopher Partridge, *The New Lion Handbook; The World's Religions* (3rd ed.; Oxford: Lion Hudson, 2005), pp134-164, 443.

Book Reviews

> Readers are invited to submit reviews of recent publications on the study of Islam and Other Faiths for possible inclusion in the CSIOF Bulletin.

The Wisdom of Islam and the Foolishness of Christianity

The Wisdom of Islam and the Foolishness of Christianity
A Christian Response to Nine Objections to Christianity by Muslim Philosophers[1]

Richard Shumack,
Island View Publishing 2014, 240pp, selected bibliography
Review by Roger Trigg[2]

This book, by Richard Shumack, who is based in Australia, confronts common objections made to Christianity by Muslim thinkers. He particularly responds to philosophical objections made by the British Muslim, Shabbir Akhtar. Shumack gives him the compliment of saying that he is 'unique among contemporary Muslim thinkers in the depth of his engagement with Christian belief.'

A basic theme is the difference, as Shumack sees it, between Christian and Muslim understanding of divine/human interaction. The Muslim, Shumack believes, sees this in terms of a 'legislative' model, according to which God lays down laws for humans through the medium of the Qur'an. Christians, on the other hand, adopt a 'fellowship' model. The first model sees God as Lord with humans as his servants, obeying His commands. The Christian model places greater stress on a personal relationship between God, as Father, and the individual believer.

---

[1] Reproduced with permission

A few words of summary cannot do justice to the complexity of the discussion, and the philosophical understanding displayed. Such dialogue between Christians and Muslims too rarely happens. There seems to be little appetite for philosophical argument amongst many Islamic scholars. On the other side, too many Western thinkers seem anxious to minimise differences between religions, and to pretend that they are even unimportant. The pluralism of the philosopher of religion, John Hick, was of this kind, and it can ultimately degenerate into a relativism that discards the idea of objective truth.

We must accept that Christianity and Islam claim truth, but both cannot be right. The doctrine of the Trinity, discussed in one of Shumack's chapters, is a case in point. Muslims may portray it as a belief in three gods and glory in a strict monotheism. Christians can say that is a misunderstanding. What cannot be allowed is the relativist conclusion that, for Muslims, God is one, but for the Christians he is a Trinity. What is true must be true for everybody, whether they accept it or not

Shumack's book is profound and readable, but raises questions. He says that 'both Christianity and Islam make the confident declaration that their respective holy books consist of the received and inerrant Word of God.' He concludes that both equally have to face the question how extant Scripture 'did originate with the testimony from God'. Yet this comparison cannot be quite right, given different Christian understandings of the role of Scripture. The Qur'an is seen as itself a direct revelation from God. The Bible, though, witnesses to such a revelation. The Qur'an is viewed as literally God's Word. The Bible points to the incarnate Logos (or Word), namely Jesus Christ. Things are not true because they are in the Bible. They are in the Bible because they are true, or so Christians believe. The latter worship a Person not a text.

A major gap in Shumack's treatment is the issue of human freedom, which he barely mentions. There are differences about this between the two religions. Christianity believes it is a God-given gift which must be respected. Human rationality is impossible without it. God wants our freely given love and adoration, and coerced belief is not genuine belief. The Western tradition of democracy springs from this basic idea. How far Islam and democracy are compatible is still unresolved. It is sometimes said, too, that Islam is more fatalist than Christianity, accepting all that happens as the will of Allah. These difficult matters remain to be debated. This book, though, illustrates that an informed and courteous interchange of views can help each religion appreciate some of the richness in the other, while still holding to their own convictions about what is true.

Professor Roger Trigg[3]

---

[3] Professor Roger Trigg is Senior Research Fellow at the Ian Ramsey Centre, University of Oxford. His latest book is *Religious Diversity: Philosophical and Political Dimensions*, Cambridge University Press, 2014

Men in Charge?: Rethinking Authority in Muslim Legal Tradition

Men in Charge?:
Rethinking Authority in Muslim Legal Tradition
Ziba Mir-Hosseini, Mulki Al-Sharmani & Jana Rumminger (eds)
Kindle edition; London: Oneworld Publications, 2015.
ISBN 978-1-78074-716-4, ISBN 978-1-78074-717-0 (ebook)

Men in Charge? is a compilation of articles by feminist Islamic scholars and the first project of *Musawah,* an Islamic feminist group launched in 2009 to give women a voice in the production of religious knowledge and legal reform.

The articles address aspects of the first part of Qur'an 4:34, which states 'Men are in charge of women by [right of] what Allah has given one over the other and what they spend [for maintenance] from their wealth' (Sahih International translation). The goal of the articles is to question and challenge Islamic family law's reliance on the traditional understanding of Q4:34 in relation to other relevant verses such as Q30:21, concerning love and affection between spouses (169/6792).

Working with the reasoning of twentieth century reformist scholars, such as Tahir al-Haddad and Fazlur Rahman, *Men in Charge?* argues that the Qur'an's eternal meaning needs to be extracted from seventh century Arabian society. Though equality was not achievable at that time, the clear trajectory of the Qur'an is towards this goal (603/6792). Therefore, a text, such as Q4:34, that implies the inferiority of women, cannot be taken on face value, as this would violate the overarching principle of equality.

In asking 'What then does it mean?', these scholars seek to ascertain what the verse would have meant to the original audience. If, as seems the case, Q4:34 was uttered in an era when women were chattels and men could do what they liked with them, then its purpose was to limit male privilege and protect female rights. In other words, Q4:34 was part of the bigger journey towards equality. Finally, the authors apply that meaning to today by asking how Islam should continue to work for equality between the sexes.

What most strikes me about this reasoning is its similarity to the way I approach the Bible. I ask the same questions: Does this verse fit with the overall message? If not, what did this verse mean in the context in which it was written? What did it mean to that original audience? Finally, what then should it mean to me?

However, not all Islamic scholars agree with this approach. Abu Mussab Wajdi Akkari describes it as audacity. 'As if Allah did not know ... the times would change.'[1]

The Islamic feminism that produced *Men in Charge?* is a relatively new phenomenon. Islamic feminist scholars of the earlier part of the twentieth century were typically dismissed as Westernised secularists. It was not until the 1980s and 90s that they managed to throw off this baggage and emerge with their own distinct voice, ready to question traditional views and approaches to the Qur'an. Some, such as Amina Wadud, have gone so far as to reject certain specific ideas in the Qur'an as no longer applicable (1528/6792). Though there is an inherent logic to such arguments, Akkari argues that Wadud is not to be taken seriously because a Muslim must believe in all the Qur'an.[2]

Strangely, the book engenders in me a sense of humility. Christianity has had its own struggle with patriarchy and still does. Taken out of its context, Ephesians 5:22 (wives submit to your husbands) sounds very similar to Qur'an 4:34 (men are in charge of women). What if it, like 4:34, had been removed from its context and used by a patriarchal society to form the basis of our marriage laws?

Isobel Lopez Ruiz in her review describes *Men in Charge?* as 'a necessary book, one which is carefully designed to combat misconceptions and prejudice, and one which, most importantly,

---

[1] Abu Mussab Wajdi Akkari "Feminist Muslims Amina Wadud" *You Tube* (18 Jan 2013) https://www.youtube.com/watch?v=gWkBISpWeJ4

[2] Akkari, "Feminist Muslims Amina Wadud."

has a practical focus: all of the book's contributors are writing for change.'[3] For me, *Men in Charge?* is a compelling combination of courage and scholarship as the book's contributors agitate for legal change and the empowerment of Muslim women.
Rebecca Hayman[4]

---

[3] Isobel Lopez Ruiz "Book Review: Men in Charge? Rethinking Authority in Muslim Legal Tradition" in London School of Economics and Political Science 14 April 2015 http://blogs.lse.ac.uk/lsereviewofbooks/2015/04/14/book-review-men-in-charge/

[4] Rebecca Hayman is a Melbourne based writer. Her latest novel *Career Advice for the Lost Soul* is a contemporary reconciliation story woven together with reflections on Luke's Gospel.

Churchill and the Islamic World

Churchill and the Islamic World

Warren Dockter
London and New York: IB Taurus, 2015
377pp including table of contents, index, bibliography and photographs

Warren Dockter, a research fellow at Cambridge University, sets out to debunk the idea that Churchill was an ignorant imperialist when it came to the Middle East and Islam. In particular, he seeks to demonstrate that Churchill's most widely quoted comment on Islam, published in *The River War* (1899):

> How dreadful are the curses which Muhammadanism[1] lays upon its votaries! Besides the fanatical frenzy, which is as dangerous in man as hydrophobia in a dog, there is this fearful fatalistic apathy...No stronger retrograde force exists in the world.

simply reflects a particularly anti-religious phase that Churchill was then going through.

Dockter demonstrates that Churchill actually had extensive experience of the Islamic world in his younger days, which included his time as a junior army officer in India and in Egypt and Sudan during Kitchener's campaign against the Mahdi. He goes on to show how Churchill was actually a great friend of the Islamic world and strove tirelessly, though ultimately unsuccessfully, to keep Turkey on the allied side during the lead up to WW1. He, perhaps rather naively, saw Turkey and the British Empire as the two powers with the world's largest Muslim populations and therefore natural allies.

---

[1] Previously the term "Muhammadanism" was used to identify the religion proclaimed by the prophet Muhammad. However, the followers of the religion preferred to identify their religion by the term "Islam" with those following the religion, as 'Muslims".

One of the most interesting aspects of this book is Dockter's demonstration of how Churchill's thinking assumed a hierarchy of civilisations. For Churchill 'religion was intrinsically linked with civilisation and progress', and he understood Christian civilisation to be at the top of this hierarchy. Churchill therefore viewed the British Empire as the pinnacle of civilisation and progress and a means of advancing civilisation, provided it lived up to these ideals. Whilst Islamic civilisations came below Christianity in Churchill's hierarchy, they were in his estimation significantly above Hindu civilisation. This at least partly explains Churchill's support for Jinnah's Muslim League in the years leading up to Indian independence, including countenancing the possibility of a separate Muslim state, which he rather naively believed would ally itself with the British Empire.

Churchill saw strong relations with Muslims in the British Empire as a means of developing strong relations with Muslims outside the empire – and as such a means of countering both Pan Islamism which at the turn of the twentieth century was beginning to emerge and the later threat of Bolshevism.

This book is an excellent analysis of the role Churchill played in relation to the major political developments that affected relations between western and Islamic countries during the periods he was in power. Yet, at the same time one feels that a number of potentially significant internal political events that occurred during this era have either been skated over or ignored completely. The Armenian genocide is only briefly mentioned, despite the author having a particular focus on Churchill's relationship with Turkey during this period. Similarly, there is no reference whatsoever to the rise of Islamism, even though The Muslim Brotherhood was certainly a potent force in Egypt during Churchill's second premiership. The latter is particularly significant as the book begins by claiming that:

> The effects of British imperial policy continue to resonate in the Islamic world and analysing its origins is crucial in understanding the current geopolitical context of the 'Arab Spring', the 'war on terror', and the rise of ISIS.

It certainly throws a very helpful light on intergovernmental relations between the West and the Islamic world at that time. This became the context for the anti-colonialism, which provided part of the seedbed within which Islamism arose. However, events such as the rise of ISIS cannot be explained without also engaging with the theological and ideological ideas that underpin radical Islamism. Dr Martin Parsons[2]

---

[2] Dr Martin Parsons worked in Afghanistan and Pakistan for a number of years, has a PhD on Islam and Christian-Muslim relations and has written extensively on Islam and politics. He is currently head of research and director of studies for an international aid agency specialising is helping Christian victims of persecution in the Islamic world.

Jesus & Muhammad

Understanding Jesus and Muhammad:
What the ancient texts say about them. [1]

Bernie Power,
Acorn Press, 161pp, table of contents, bibliography, tables, diagrams, pictures.

Sensibly discussing Islam is obviously a great need for the Australian public in general, and Christians in particular. Sensationalist views of Muslims, both positive and negative dominate our media, Islamist terrorism is the prime target for our security forces, and Muslim refugees bear the brunt of much political debate over our immigration policies. Properly, Christians play a key role in welcoming and advocating for these refugees and, increasingly, are seeking to engage with Muslims in discussions to do with faith. Also properly, Christians seek this engagement for both missional and community building reasons.

Discourse about Islam, however, is often hindered by the fact that few ordinary Australians – Christians and Muslims alike – have a deep knowledge of Islam's authoritative texts. Many will not be aware that the traditional Islamic schools of thought constructed their theologies via appeal to not only the Qur'an (understood as the word of God), but also the *hadith* (the traditions to do with Muhammad's words and actions), and the authoritative biography of Muhammad by Ibn Ishaq. Coming to terms with this is crucial, especially with the growing prominence of groups like ISIS who are *salafist*. (Salafism is a traditionalist reform movement that seeks to return Islam to its supposedly pristine early form as witnessed in the hadith and biography). It is, however, rare to meet even a keen Muslim who has a solid familiarity with the hadith, and even rarer to meet one who has read Ibn Ishaq's biography.

---

[1] First published in *Crucible*, Vol. 7, No. 1, May 2016 and reprinted here with permission.

This situation clearly makes it difficult to have constructive conversations on Islam, and it is this that has led Melbourne School of Theology's Dr Bernie Power to write *Understanding Jesus and Muhammad: What the ancient texts say about them*. Power is uniquely qualified to help Muslims and Christians talk. He lived and worked in the Muslim world for many years, and, uniquely among Christians as far as I know, pursued doctoral research into the *hadith* traditions. His expertise is well recognized with regular invitations to teach at Muslim universities.

As the title suggests, *Understanding Jesus and Muhammad* is built upon the crucial, and sensible, idea that Islam (and Christianity) cannot be properly understood without reference to its foundational texts. From this starting point Power offers a comparison between Jesus and Muhammad that covers a whole range of topics that regularly arise in conversation between Christians and Muslims. All the usual suspects are here: what the Qur'an says about Jesus and what the Bible (supposedly) says about Muhammad; the place of religious violence in the life and teachings of Muhammad/Jesus; human rights as taught and exemplified by Muhammad/Jesus; and the treatment of women by both. Less common, but nevertheless important, topics such as the miraculous, eschatology and the precise nature of faith are covered along the way.

The aim here is that particular Muslim/Christian beliefs about these things are evaluated by examining what each faith's key texts have to say and then seeing if it stands up to theological or historical scrutiny. The book is unusual in its style of going about this. Most chapters begin with a brief story to introduce the topic. From that point on there are lots of dot points, lists of references, diagrams and summaries. This is not a weakness, rather it is a strength. That's because this is designed as a book to be used, rather than read. It is, in short, a handbook for discussion that summarises the key things you need to know about each topic including what responses you will likely get to different points. It is worth the price for the volume of information packed into the summary charts and diagrams alone.

What Power has produced, then, is not so much a short text book to be read for information, but instead a "handbook" to be used in facilitating discourse. Since the material here was forged in the context of real life interaction by Power over many years, the discussions are framed in everyday language, and have been road tested for facilitating helpful conversations.

Taken as a handbook, *Understanding Jesus and Muhammad* is a great resource for any Christian who is speaking about faith with Muslims. I recognize each and every conversation from my many years of living, working and playing among Muslim friends. Muslim readers, though, may not be so enthusiastic. This is not because the book contains false or misleading material. Power knows his stuff on both Christianity and Islam, and even in such a short popular book, his scholarly expertise is evident. Nevertheless, it is fair to say that, despite every effort at objectivity, Power writes as a Christian who has decided that in the apologetic debate between Islam and Christianity, the argument clearly falls on the side of Christ. It is hard to blame Power for this honesty, but I would recommend that, at the very least, any Christian engaging with Islam read a similar work by a Muslim writer to hear the other side of the debate in their own words. Power's bibliography is easily comprehensive enough to show you where to look for such works.

One quibble the Christian reader might have with *Understanding Jesus and Muhammad* is that some of Power's illustrations of complex Christian doctrines are oversimplified for the sake of contextualising his point for a Muslim audience. While Power's motivation is understandable and commendable, it remains theologically problematic to, for example, illustrate the Trinity using mathematics or the chemistry of water. This is, however, a small quibble. *Understanding Muhammad and Jesus* is an excellent resource worth having on your shelf and, indeed, in your backpack, ready to pull out at university or on the bus. As Australia comes to terms with Islam, and especially radical Islamism, Christians should be leading the way. We are among the few left in our rapidly secularising society – and especially our rapidly simplifying and polarising media – who can genuinely understand people who are motivated by theological conviction. More importantly, we are the only ones who can respond to Islamism's theo-political ideology with a theological alternative, in the gospel, that can properly satisfy the misplaced zeal of Muslims for God. This book will equip you better to do just that.
Dr Richard Shumack[2]

---

[2] Director, Arthur Jeffery Centre for the Study of Islam, Melbourne School of Theology

CSIOF News and Activities

New Name:

As from 26th April, 2016 the Centre for the Study of Islam and Other Faiths at the Melbourne School of Theology changed its name to the Arthur Jeffery Study for the Study of Islam. Over the past nine years, the focus of the Centre has increasingly gravitated to the study of Islam which has prompted the name change. Dr Richard Shumack is the Director of the Centre. Dr Peter Riddell, the former Director, handed over the responsibility to Dr Shumack at the beginning of 2015.

Publications:

CSIOF Occasional Papers, No 5, 2015

Faiths in Conversation; Comparative themes in and Perspectives across the Religions consists of a series of essays where in most cases the teachings of two religions are examined in relation to a topic. For example: Death and Dying in Hinduism and Islam; The Interconnection between Buddhism and Chinese Religions; Islam and Judaism; From Eastern Religions to New Age Religions.

It is now available for purchase through amazon.com or book depository. If you have any queries or questions, please contact info@JefferyCentre.mst.edu.au.

CSIOF Events

Pastors and Christian Leaders Seminar
Monday 19th September, 7:30pm, MST, Burwood Highway, Wantirna. Dr Sasan Tavassoli, originally from Iran, is the quest speaker. It will be followed by the book launch of Elizabeth Kendal's latest publication, *After Saturday, comes Sunday*.

Research Fellow, The Centre for Public Christianity

Understanding and Answering Islam Conference in conjunction with Ravi Zacharias International Ministries,
7th-8th April, 2017

Please contact the Arthur Jeffery Centre for the Study of Islam, Melbourne School of Theology for further information about these events. info@JefferyCentre.mst.edu.au.

Post Graduate Seminars
Three students who are associated with the CSIOF/Arthur Jeffery Centre for the Study of Islam will be presenting seminars at various times during the year. Each of these students is from overseas. For two of them English is their second language which adds to the challenges of making a presentation.

GLOSSARY

Term	Description
Caliph	The successor to Muhammad as political and military ruler of the Islamic community
Dar al-Islam	The House of Islam; areas where Islam has political dominance
Dar al-Harb	The House of War; the rest of the world not under Islam
Da'wa	Mission
Dhimmi	"Protected" non-Muslim communities (Second class citizens)
Durura	Necessity
Fasiq	Sinner
Hadith	Authoritative traditions of all that Muhammad words and deeds
Hajj	Pilgrimage (to Mecca)
Hijra	Migration
Huda	Guidance
Ijtihad	Process of legal deduction by which a scholar produces a legal opinion
Imam	(Sunni meaning) Leader of congregational prayer in mosque as well as a community leader (Shia meaning) A person of spiritual authority and importance; also refers to a number of recognised leaders (General use) A recognised Muslim scholar
Jahiliyya	Paganism/ Ignorance
Jihad *Jehad*	Holy war; "a continuous and never-ending struggle waged on all fronts including political,

Term	Description
	economic, social, psychological, domestic, moral and spiritual." [Malite, p54]
Jinn	Demon/ spiritual being
Jizya	"Tax" if not converting to Islam
Kafir	Unbeliever/ disbeliever/ infidel
Maslaha	Public good
Mujaddid	Renewer of Islam
Mujahiddin	Holy warriors
Mu'min	Believer
Nur	Light
Saracens	Name Christians used for Muslims initially
Seerah	Biography of Muhammad
Shahada	Repeating "There is no God but God (Allah) and Muhammad is his messenger"
Sunna	Way or example of Muhammad
Sura	Chapter of the Qur'an
Tafsirs	Qur'anic commentaries
Tahrif	Corruption, distortion (of text)
Taqlid	Imitation of judgments made by earlier scholars
Tawhid	Oneness of Allah (Sufi meaning) Oneness with Allah
Umma	One Muslim community worldwide
Zakat	Almsgiving at the mosque (Sufi meaning) Totally giving oneself to Allah and to a Sufi brotherhood

Notes for Contributors

Submission requirements:

Manuscript

Papers should be 1000-1500 words, with a maximum of 1500. Papers with more than 1500 words will not be considered.

Submissions prepared in Microsoft Word format are preferred.

All papers are to be written in English, and an English transliteration given to any quotations or short phrases in original language.

Authors are advised to use gender inclusive and non-discriminatory language.

Any visuals should be integrated into the document, or sent separately as separate jpg or gif files with an explanation as to their position in the paper.

Footnotes should follow the style used in previous issues of the Bulletin. If footnotes are used, do not include a bibliography. When including a bibliography only cite works mentioned in the paper.

When quoting or referring to an internet site add the date on which the item was cited. For example www.reference cited dd/mm/yy. This is necessary as internet sites can change.

Submission

Papers to be considered for inclusion are to be submitted directly to the Editor.

Submissions are to be forwarded via electronic mail to info@JefferyCentre.mst.edu.au . If submitting within Australia; a hard copy must also be posted to Arthur Jeffery Centre, Melbourne School of Theology, PO Box 6257 Vermont Sth., Vic 3133.

A declaration that the submitted articles are your own work and that you've acknowledged the work/s of others used in the articles in the references, etc. must be included with any submission.

A covering letter that includes the authors' names, titles and affiliations, together with complete mailing addresses, including email, telephone and facsimile numbers should be attached to the paper.

Review of Submissions

All submissions will be sent to referees for anonymous recommendation.

The Editor holds the right to make editorial corrections to accepted submissions.

Copyright

The CSIOF Bulletin is published by the Melbourne School of Theology Press. The copyright for any published papers will remain with the author. MST publishes these papers on the following conditions:

- They do not appear elsewhere (including web pages) for 180 days from the date of publication in the CSIOF Bulletin.
- Whenever they are printed elsewhere (including web pages), the following notice will be included: "This article first appeared in the __ issue, date of the CSIOF Bulletin series".

The CSIOF\MST retains the right to use the paper in any of the CSIOF publications, whether reprint or in some electronic form (i.e. Online),

The CSIOF\MST retains the right to use a portion or description of the paper with your name in our promotional material.

Authors are themselves responsible for obtaining permission to reproduce copyright material from other sources.

The author will be presented with one copy of the publication.

Disclaimer

The opinions and conclusions published in the CSIOF Bulletin series are those of the authors and do not necessarily represent the views of the Editor or the CSIOF. The CSIOF Bulletin serves purely as an information medium, to inform interested parties of religious trends, discussion and debates. The Bulletin does not intend in any way to actively promote hatred of any religion or its followers.

www.ingramcontent.com/pod-product-compliance
Lightning Source LLC
Chambersburg PA
CBHW070628300426
44113CB00010B/1706